That's Where You Go
&
Other Short Stories

Peter J. Dellolio

ISBN: 978-93-6354-312-6

First Edition: 2025
Rs. 500/-

Cyberwit.net
HIG 45 Kaushambi Kunj, Kalindipuram
Allahabad - 211011 (U.P.) India
http://www.cyberwit.net
Tel: +(91) 9415091004
E-mail: info@cyberwit.net

Printed at Repro India Limited.

For Kip

More than a brother, more than a friend

Contents

That's Where You Go

Early morning. Crisp autumn of the schoolyard. Beginning of the school day. Donna's father crouches. Squatting he points. To guide Donna. Long high wall. Blocking October sun. In front of the wall Donna's father. Gray and shadows and dark brick and Donna looking straight. The door. Brown entrance door. Moments for others. Immeasurable length of time inside Donna's mind. Crispness from shadow. Morning October umbrage. Full sun when it falls upon the pavement. A faint reminder of summer. Just beyond late summer. Its warmth captured in early October school mornings. Donna looking. Feeling resentful to need her father pointing. Feeling proud to show her father she remembered. Car horns intermittent. Parents leaving. Pebbles scraping on pavement. Bits of glass. Crunch under school shoe leather. Quick to praise. Forever patient. Admiring his daughter. For trying on these mornings. Donna's father in dreams sees the schoolyard. The brown door. The high wall keeping faint warmth away from the concrete. Seeing himself kneeling. Gently holding his uncertain daughter. Feeling the eyes of teachers upon him. Feeling the sting of their pitying eyes. Knowing he brings a burden to them each day. Knowing that on all of the different days there are always the same conversations. Words spoken not too close to him. Words spoken not too far that he cannot hear parts of what is said. Teachers and parents. School aides and counselors. He hears their voices in his dreams. He hears them speak. Talking about the tragedy of Donna. No special place for her. Not in this day and age. Bureaucracy of the mid-century public school system. Prohibiting special treatment. Donna must remain. The same fourth grade class. Same as the other children. The normal children. Donna's father never uses that word. He never says "normal" in her presence. Nothing helps. Nothing restores what was carefree in her. Nothing reactivates the laughter. Of her infancy.

He alternates between helpless weeping and monstrous rage. He weeps only when he is alone. At home. When his wife is shopping. When Donna is at school. His primordial anger bursts across the steering wheel that he pounds. Driving home after dropping Donna off at school. Stopping at traffic lights. Striking the wheel. The fleshy side of his palm turning numb. Donna smiles in his dreams. They run along the shore. The zenith of summer creates true heat and energy. There is nothing in heaven or nature to separate him from Donna. There are no trapdoors of fate or tragedy through which his hopes for Donna must fall. There is no well of infinite depth to swallow and imprison even the smallest of his aspirations for her. Gulls, elegant whitish gray aviators, gracefully circle frolicking father and daughter. Iridescent shells everywhere. She picks up each one and names its color. Spells each word. Recites the alphabet. Names the capitals of the American states. Names all the Presidents since Washington. Then it is morning. It is the new school year. Donna's father is pointing. She leans against him. Fingers in mouth. Eyes wide trying. Wanting and trying. Her father says, "That's where you go."

* * *

now it's friday go to grandma's where's the pretzels I want a pretzel with the milk wait oh no I don't have any money look over there donna bought hers sucking it staring at it she's not normal why is she like that always smelling her fingers her glasses are so thick never looks like she knows where she is I don't think I ever saw her laugh or anything like that sometimes I hear mom talking over coffee to a couple of the mothers of the kids from down the street talking over coffee and I can hear them in my room they say donna is mentally handicapped I had to ask what that meant I thought it was that she was in an accident but she doesn't need crutches or anything oh I wanted a pretzel really bad I like that grandma lives on mulberry street it's near chinatown lots of lights in the windows of all the markets and souvenir stores and restaurants I like to smell all the incense in the stores there's lots of colored paper lanterns and little dragon figures I like to look at the boxes of incense sometimes they have tiny cones of solid incense packed in rows like a bunch of wizard hats and I can play in the park tomorrow why such weird glasses and nothing about the class seems to get her attention she flips her notebook pages so fast like there's something secret to find I don't know it's not like the rest of us I want to eat something now oh why didn't I remember to ask mom the teacher had to help donna yesterday when we did the art tracing all the leaves starting to fall so many nice colors and big ones I found some really big ones they haven't all gotten dry yet we traced the leaves with the construction paper on top of them rubbed the fat flat crayons back and forth making the veins come out from the leaf but donna kept ripping her paper she used the crayon edge and she rubbed too hard she was very rough with the paper why she didn't just do it like the rest of us it was really pretty easy just rub back and forth back and forth keep rubbing the flat part of the crayon to get the leaf traced donna must have made mistakes three or four times she had ripped papers on her desk some of the kids looked I guess she was embarrassed she took them off her desk and stuffed them into her book bag then she tried again she kept trying to do it the right way

All of the children assembling in rows and columns in the early morning. In the crisp autumn of the schoolyard. It is the beginning of the school day; Donna's father crouches; as usual, she is confused. So after squatting he points as patiently and gently as he can. He must do this to guide Donna so that she will go in the right direction and enter the building through the right door. There is a long high wall behind Donna's father. It blocks the early October sun from spreading at least a modicum of warmth across the schoolyard pavement. In front of the wall, focused on his daughter's mixture of disorientation and fleeting attention, Donna's father moves his arm with the gray sweater and, pointing for his daughter, shadows and dark brick seem to secure the two of them in a tableau of light charcoal shade. Fingers in mouth, looking straight but without lucid memory, Donna nods, eyes wide, trying to connect the location of the brown school door with her father's soothing gesture and calming words. Donna's entire existence is, of course, a matter of perpetual wanting and trying. There is no impatience or abject pity in her father's regard of her permanent mental limitations. He strives at all times to show her that he believes she can succeed. It is not only a father's love. The man fervently subscribes to the notion that those unfortunate enough to be born with emotional and intellectual handicaps deserve all the respect and encouragement one can give. Unfortunately, Donna's temperament is such that unprovoked hostility and a stubborn streak of irrational anger are never far from the surface of her thoughts, actions, and words. Yet, in all fairness, no one who lives in the world she cannot inhabit, who does not participate in her painful mental life, can truly know how difficult her struggles must be. She wants her father to know that she understands his words ("That's where you go"). That is what her father says, each time, on these school day mornings.

just sits there staring sucking her pretzel but it's like she's not really here like awake but not really never talks to anyone glad it's friday tonight we'll have chinese food at grandma's so hungry now I forgot to ask mom for change this morning what would happen should I try maybe ask donna for some pretzel I see her father in the mornings all the time while he's squatting with her and pointing to the main entrance where her class has to go but she gets to stay with him until it's time to go in I guess he wants her to feel good I see the parents talking about her no one ever looks at donna's father it's like they pretend he's not there they all look like they are embarrassed when he leaves the schoolyard after donna finally goes into the entrance sometimes she looks back at her father to wave goodbye and he always waves back with a smile and waits until she goes in before he leaves the schoolyard I like fridays because fridays are always chinese food at grandma's and when it's the beginning of school like the first week the way it is now it's still almost light out when mom and I get to the chinese restaurant to pick up the food there's a big window by the bar at the front of the restaurant where we wait and I like to watch all the store lights and the street lights go on because it starts to get dark by then it's night time when we go back around the corner to grandma's building carrying the food

So this image of Donna standing while looking and Donna's father crouching while pointing is a tableau quite familiar to the students and the teachers assembling in the schoolyard. The rows and columns of students ready to go inside; the crisp autumn of the early morning. It is the beginning of the new school season. Donna's father crouches as usual. Which door is the right one? Donna is still confused after her father squats and holds her gently from behind. The distance between Donna and the door is always the same; the direction in which Donna's father points is always the same; the long high wall behind Donna's father is always the same; the early October sun blocked by the wall is always the same. There are times when the students hurrying into another school entrance, watching this tableau and feeling chilly, miss the temporary October warmth blocked by the high wall and kept away from the schoolyard pavement. There is an unspoken yearning for the recently ended summer. But there is also the excitement of the new school year. A strange, paradoxical mixture of lament over the loss of vacation freedom and the happy ascension to the next grade, the welcome faces of friends who live in different neighborhoods and haven't been seen since June, and the compelling morning energy that somehow provides the children with a rush of interest in the continuation of their academic lives. The high wall keeps a large section of the schoolyard in shadow. Acting like an emotional border, it separates the counterfeit warmth of the October sun from the realization that the heat of the real summer is indeed over. Every child in the schoolyard has this feeling, to one degree or another. For young children coming out of the dreamy cocoon of their summertime fantasies, congregating in the schoolyard during this first week of school, there is a kind of therapeutic camaraderie, the way family members and cherished friends try to comfort one another at the wake of a beloved soul. The children mourned the loss of their summer in this way. They sought solace and comfort in one another's company. Sadly, for Donna, there was nothing in the character of her facial expression, or her demeanor, or her voice that reflected even the most microscopic awareness of these feelings. The weary emptiness in her eyes betrayed no recognition or acknowledgement of the psychological gestalt of the situation. It would have made no difference if Donna were standing alone in a foul wilderness or surrounded by the pleasures and beauty of paradise. Her expression would have remained the same.

from the golden dragon I'll go with mom we go around seven to pick it up hmmm I really love the hot mustard in that soup donna stares like she is somewhere else I think I'll ask her just want a little piece break off a piece at the end all she has to do break it off with the round thin slices of pork and then some beef with oyster sauce she could snap it I guess I could ask anita but she's still up front getting her pretzels she sits in the next desk behind donna and I also like the beef with oyster sauce dish really like all the sauce on my rice but it's not really from oysters I guess they just call it that for a name I couldn't eat it if that was true I mean really made from oysters they're shell fish I can't eat shell fish because of an allergy and I'm going to have to turn around and face the blackboard soon the milk and pretzels are almost all given out all I had to do was ask mom for change I like all those little shops that we pass on our way to pick up the food there's so many fish and meat places they are all next to stone steps that go down there are basements all over the block they look kind of scary all dark and a little smelly and in the shops they do these things I don't understand there's all these cooked ducks all dark brown hanging in a row from hooks right in front of the big shop windows their heads are still connected but their eyes are closed and their beaks point in different directions when donna walks it's like there's a wind or something that moves her the way she swings her book bag she even stumbles sometimes but nothing is there she's just awkward moving the way the wind gives you a little push when it's really strong in the winter

It was natural that this daily tableau of Donna looking absently while being held gently by her father pointing steadily would remind some of the students of pictures they had seen, photographs in books of statues of angels in cemeteries, pointing upward, or statues of George Washington, in parks, pointing forward. It may have been that the collective memories and imaginations of the students, the parents, and every other adult connected with the school, used this sameness of Donna and her father, the schoolyard mornings, and the angles of the shadows, to mentally construct a kind of pure visual permanence, an irreducibility of imagery that somehow lingered in their minds, as they mingled or stood apart, observing the dual presence of Donna and her father. As they made their way into the school, they were completely baffled by the power of this imagery, of something so mundane and unchanging. That power created a primitive social element that became embedded within their group consciousness. In an anthropological sense, it negated all other aspects of recollection and understanding, as if no basis for knowing Donna and her father was possible other than the communal status of these shared perceptions and memories of Donna looking and her father pointing. The summers between school years nurtured this subconscious process. Those students who lived in the same neighborhoods had ample opportunities to play together. They would invariably share stories about Donna's strangeness. Yet the only common ingredient in any of these narratives was the mythological component of Donna and her father as a self-contained image. Donna was always looking and her father was always pointing. One of these students was a boy in Donna's class, the one who teased her about the pretzel, who pretended that he had taken a piece of her pretzel when it was his other neighbor, Anita, who had given him a piece of her pretzel, and who, by fooling Donna this way, had caused her to become most agitated and upset, to reach out in anguish, to reclaim what she believed to be her stolen property, aggressively exclaiming "Gimmmmmeeeee!" in a tortured howl of anger, until Anita, trying to ameliorate and soothe the situation, hurriedly explained to Donna that it was she who had shared some of her pretzel with the boy, demonstrating the fact by showing the remaining pretzel to Donna. Approximately two inches were missing. Apparently, several minutes before, the boy had asked Donna for a piece of her pretzel. Without looking in his direction, staring off as if the boy wasn't there, Donna adamantly shook her head, saying blankly, "No, get your own."

like everybody else there's something wrong donna sure doesn't talk or act like us it's weird it's like she needs all her concentration just to do the easiest things mom even asked me do you need anything I said no and we kissed then I had to get in line it was almost time to go inside we all looked at donna and her father one more time before we went inside it was just something that everybody did because all the lines of the students had moved up and the teachers usually told us not to stare at them stupid that I forgot I could have gotten change from her right there so hungry now I have that burning feeling in my stomach I really hate that and there's anita up front getting her milk donna staring and sucking I wonder if she even sees all of us maybe she doesn't even know where she is who we are like somebody in what they call a trance like I saw in a spooky movie over the weekend I really love to mix that mustard in the won ton soup then the soup turns brown from the last time I went with mom that nice chinese lady was there her name is francis she's the owner very friendly to me she talks to mom while we wait for the order to come out of the kitchen I guess I have what the grown ups call a crush on francis she talks to me like I'm a young man even though I'm only a kid she's very pretty but has a few patches of gray in her hair she doesn't seem too old maybe it's because she's not much taller than me I liked that for some reason and I liked that she always wore gray dresses she spoke very quietly I guess because she was being polite and also not to bother the people at the tables near the bar

So this early morning represented, for this early period of her life, and for the rest of her life, all of the trials and frustrations and confusion and anger that, for Donna, were the inherent characteristics of her mental disability. It may be that, after bringing Donna to the same spot on so many occasions, her father often dreamt of the crisp autumn of the schoolyard, when Donna was most frightened, because of the new classes and different teachers and the overall anxiety of the beginning of the school day. It may be that, in his dreams, Donna's father felt a sense of pride in his protection of Donna, that the high wall did not prevent the early October sun from spreading a few final layers of warmth upon the schoolyard and the students and the teachers, and that the sharp black blocks and angles of shapes of shadow that were only he pointing and Donna looking, had assumed the heroic contours of some great act, some kind of majestic signature of humanity.

"Donna's father crouches like that every day, showing her where to go," whispered the art teacher to one of the mothers standing close by.

"I know," the mother replied, "and every time I see him squatting he points to the same door. What a patient man. Such a shame with that little girl. Maybe she ought to be in a special school?"

"I thought that, too. It's so hard on her teacher, I mean these classes are up to thirty children and that's hard enough. A classroom full of fussy, frantic ten year olds! And then to try to get through to a child like that. You know, I've never seen that girl Donna smile. It's like she's a bitter old woman sometimes."

"I know what you mean. It's not fair to the teacher or the school. Not to disrespect the poor girl, and her family, after all, look at what that man does for her, every morning. But there should be something else in the public school system, something that's designed to work for children like that."

"It's really a shame. I don't know if it's a birth defect or what. She's obviously mentally handicapped but not beyond reach, I mean, she does talk, she seems like she can do some of the homework assignments. But I can tell you: she keeps to herself like an old maid praying in church. Nothing friendly about that child at all," the art teacher declared as she finished muttering her observations to the mother, not wanting anyone nearby to hear her words, although the schoolyard was very noisy with shouting children, the scuffing of the leather soles of their dress shoes on the concrete, the staccato beeping of car horns as some parents drove off after saying goodbye to their child, and the nasal, intermittent bells signaling that it was almost time to go inside.

I saw something on television about what they say are emotionally disturbed people I asked mom what that meant because I didn't really understand what they were talking about I thought when you disturbed someone they were usually busy concentrating on something and donna never seemed able to concentrate for more than a few seconds then she almost always became angry but mom explained that we should have respect and sympathy for people like that because emotionally disturbed meant being lost or trapped sometimes and everyday things are a thousand times harder to understand for someone like that and the last time I saw francis it was a busy friday night it was the first time she couldn't really stay by the bar at the front of the restaurant to talk with me and mom people kept coming in she took these dark maroon menus from behind the bar and walked the people over to their tables mom said don't bother francis now she's busy I thought maybe it meant crazy I knew that word from before but mom said no and not to ever say that to donna it would not be sensitive or polite to say that word I wanted those circular thin pieces of pork I think I'm going to ask donna what's the worst that could happen maybe she will say I can have a piece of pretzel I don't know for sure it's the soft restaurant lights that make the red lipstick francis wears look so real I mean real like flowers she's a really pretty lady I told mom I don't want to ever make donna feel bad so I was glad mom explained about what it all meant because it was really strong mustard they called it the house mustard I don't know why but when I put too much in my soup my eyes burned a little and my nose dripped a bit I liked it there was something nice about having that next spoonful and getting that tingle in my nose

To give Donna a kind of emotional prosthetic of security and reassurance, to guide Donna in his usual position beside the long high wall, day after day, school year after school year, these humble, self-sacrificing tasks bestowed purpose and grace upon Donna's father. They became his reasons for living. It was this almost iconic image of Donna's father, in front of the wall that was always blocking October sun, crouching behind his daughter who was always agitated, confused, and angry, that teachers and students, attendants and aides, put into the mental storage of abstract imagery, an image that somehow possessed a kind of dignified autonomy, a majestic spirit, like the sight of a forest or a dam or a river. The effect of this image was such that it left an indelible impression upon the minds and memory of all those at the school who saw it. Each of them, as the years passed, in various stages of their lives, by crouching to do something in a certain way or feeling a momentary chill in early October sun, would experience a flash thought of recollection, smiling a little more wisely each year, their souls enriched by the lessons of time, and their minds seeing Donna's father performing those endless rituals of protection. The unpredictable aggressiveness that sometimes accompanies mentally hindered people was certainly prevalent in Donna. Whether provoked or cajoled, she could often be nasty and mean. Of course, everyone had empathy for the sight of Donna staring blankly, fingers in mouth, eyes wide trying to identify the door that her poor father must have pointed at hundreds of times. In the sweater he always wore, creating the same reassuring image of gray and shadows, by the high wall and dark brick and Donna always looking, wanting (to go to the right door) and trying (to remember while her father pointed).

why is she yelling like that hope I don't get into trouble good thing the teacher is in the hall I was just making believe I guess I shouldn't have teased donna like that just wanted to get even with her for being so stingy I only asked her for a tiny piece of pretzel and she didn't even look at me just kept shaking her head saying to go get my own and then when she wasn't looking and Anita was coming back with her milk and her two pretzel sticks I asked her and she gave me some right away she's nice but then after she went to her desk behind donna I turned around to show donna the pretzel and made it seem as though I took it from her she got so excited and upset I didn't want to make her get so afraid that some of her pretzel was missing and anita even felt bad about it she called out from behind she said no donna I gave it to him see look and she held out the pretzel where she broke some off at the bottom what's wrong with donna why is she so upset over things like that

*   *   *

It is Donna's twentieth birthday. Pointing to the bus stop, her father still says, "That's where you go."

Leading her away from the toy store, he thought of the phrase he had uttered so many times when Donna went to elementary school. *That's where you go.* As he pulled Donna away, this recollection made him realize that, although a twenty year old, mature woman, Donna was now no more emotionally and psychologically evolved than she was on those school mornings from the past: forever lost in her own world of petulance, confusion, and dysfunction. The intervening years brought no deliverance. There were no miracles for this daughter cherished by a father who had been so wearied by misfortune and chaos. The gulls used their beaks to penetrate the underbelly of blue and dark green crabs. They tore out the flesh, gulped it down, and flew up again, looking for their next hapless target. There was no beauty in it. The mechanical precision of their hunting skills was accompanied by total indifference to the fate of their prey. They did what nature had programmed them to do. Donna was having a tantrum over something she had seen in the window of the toy store. There was a little birthday party arranged for her at home. Some relatives and friends were already there, so Donna's father wanted to get back. He refused to buy the toy; there were many gifts waiting for Donna and it was getting late. Holding his daughter's wrist, rushing towards the bus stop, digging for tokens with his other hand, Donna's father failed to notice his tall, strong daughter placing her foot in his way. She was angry and upset that he did not buy the toy. As usual, she couldn't suppress her nasty impulses, her desire to retaliate against her father with all the self-absorption of a bratty child. She wanted to trip her father; she wanted him to fall. Because of Donna's silence, no one would know the truth; she would never reveal anything about the accident she caused, resulting in an injury that would ultimately take her father's life. He fell, hitting his head on the concrete, resulting in a massive heart attack because of his life-long cardiac condition. He would go into a coma and die within several days. By expressing her anger over not getting the toy, Donna was demonstrating her resentment like young children committing rebellious acts of violence. Reacting on that primitive level of behavior, Donna thought her hostility towards her father was innocent and harmless. She did not intend to kill him. She would never fully understand that she caused his death.

Sitting next to her father as he lay dying on the street, Donna thought she heard someone calling for an ambulance. Many loud sirens were screeching inside Donna's head. She was staring at something, her fingers in her mouth, her eyes wide. The words her father spoke seemed to be mixing in her mind with the repeating ambulance noise.

...nee-naw...nee-naw...That's where you go...nee-naw...That's where you go...nee-naw...

nee-naw...That's where...nee-naw...you go...nee-naw...nee-naw...nee-naw...nee-naw...

A CAPE FOR THE PRINCESS

that's what they say that you can hear them screaming every night all through the night as if they

take turns first it's the ones down the hall then it's the ones a few floors up all the horrific screams that reach out to a world that does not listen they are the ones who have no one they are not visited they were committed it was a time when someone could be left in a place like that until they died there were no laws or medical protocol to stop it there is a great pity in it there is a sombre feeling unlike anything in the daily lives of the sane nothing is like that subterranean isolation nothing is like that separation from ordinary life screaming every night all through the night as if they take turns first it's the ones a few floors down then it's the ones a few floors up a chanting of communal sorrow like the baying of lost dogs on a hill in the moonlight not knowing where they are not knowing where to go do these people in these white gowns behind these white steel doors remember who they used to be who they lived with who they worked with in another time it was another life as if that life were a dream that each of them awoke from finding themselves here treated as though they are vegetal specimens in a botanical laboratory nothing behind their staring eyes except a secret hollow cry of remembrance of what they used to do in lives far removed from the smell of ammonia the stench of dried vomit the squeak of wheelchairs the unimaginable loneliness that crawls out of every corner and every shadow swallowing their feeble moments of faint recollection there is an old man who stomps around his room he bangs violently on the metal guards over the windows of his room there is nothing there except a mattress he spreads his excrement over the walls across the floor he was a school teacher long ago *mathematics!* he shouts as the attendants bathe him a shave in the bathtub he tries to drink the dirty bathtub water it is like a majestic beast captured deprived of its dignity and freedom having one last moment when it remembers what it could do a cry of recognition of having been that is the way the old man utters like a flash thought of recognition a fiber of memory coming back to someone lost in the abyss of Alzheimers it is the tiniest fractional glimpse into what was what happened what is no more *mathematics!* there is even a moment of humor *is it on the house?* he asks as the attendant offers him a drink from the hose a drink of fresh water maybe this is a grand illusion a magician's trickery a conjuror's incantation from some faraway time and there are those few precious moments when they think it was all a mistake my mother is coming for me my husband is waiting in the car to take me home these are the tragic pulsations of their hopeless thoughts only to be returned once again to this world of sorrow and confusion sometimes the sonority of the screams and shouts is replaced by sobbing an unimaginably sorrowful chorus of weeping one would think that they had seen the end of the world or were being tormented by demons prodding them humiliating them confusing them destroying the tiny grip on reality that they occasionally show it is an inhuman cry an utterly inhuman cry

*

She loved to play. To make believe she was a princess. That was her greatest fun. It was so natural to pretend. After all, that is the sovereign realm of all children. Their imaginations are the epitome of innocent invention. No one could see at this early stage that soon irrational fantasy and dangerous mental preoccupations would take over her sweet life. In a few short years she would begin to hallucinate. Hear voices. See things. Become antagonistic and violent. It was heartbreaking for her parents to witness such a grotesque transformation. She loved to take the sheet from her parent's bed. She dragged it into her little room. Wrapped it around herself. Then she was the princess. Then she had the cape meant only for the princess. She walked slowly up and down in her room. It was the solemn ceremony of the princess entering her castle. Look at all the rose petals laid before her feet! She is the princess. Her cape is magnificent. It is a sacred coronation. Attendants are bringing her the scepter. The King and Queen beam at her with admiration and pride. They are so proud of her. Knowing how much she loves the prince. Wanting them to be married and to be happy. The Queen whispers in the King's ear. She's hoping they will have twins. The King has decreed that their wedding day will become an official holiday for the village. No taxes will be collected and the people do not have to perform their duties or their labors. He is very pleased about his daughter's wedding. He has granted her wish to let all the townspeople attend the wedding ceremony and for each of them to receive a gold coin and a dozen roses. The King is a very gracious man. He loves his daughter.

*

Sorrow dragged night glaring exam room nothing. Caught inside thoughts no more. Flash of terror strapped down. Bed sheet orderlies rough ripped away stains and stench. Leather cuffs now fastened quickly mouthpiece thick stiff rubber. Ammonia smell alcohol lingering antiseptic attack a violence of being forced. Big nurses each side holding her head in place. *Look at all the rose petals laid before her feet!* Not a princess demons dance schizophrenic Hell all thinking fiery monster puzzles. Cacophony wells black water cries unheard. Hidden burial childhood dancing fun crippled. Inside her mixtures moments rough shifts. Inside her all deformed her parents sobbing. Throbbing always scorched remnants. Not to return. Mind locked away vast jagged feelings. Swirling thoughts all uproar. All fractured becoming less. Always becoming less no reason accumulation. Nothing forward. Fractured. Nothing beyond all clouds thick thoughts darkness. Taken robbed defiled childhood energy space enveloped madness wins. Madness. She wanders not inside joy.

*

nothing is like that subterranean isolation nothing is like that separation from ordinary life screaming every night all through the night as if they take turns first it's the ones a few floors up then it's the ones down the hall it as if the attendants and the doctors and the nurses treat them like mannequins there is no longer the simple dignity of human beings interacting with each other take this one there put that one in the chair give the other one a bath nothing is more dehumanizing than being regarded and treated like an object to the staff these lost souls are nothing more than animated dummies if restraints are required the patients are summarily strapped into their beds or on the exam tables the thick dark leather stained with bodily fluids the lightning white flash of fluorescent light a cyclops of bulbs hovering over the heads of the thrashing and shouting and sobbing figures writhing in an unspeakably contorted manner as if thousands of scorpions were racing through their blood vessels mocking the lost freedom of the patients' bodies the waves of involuntary spasms shock treatment that chases away the razor blades waging war inside their minds but also erases the weeping self trembling inside trying to regain shreds of memory that are no longer visible no longer alive people who have been dragged away by shrieking hooded rapists of electricity a young man tries to speak to the head psychiatrist *this is harming me! it's harming me!* he repeats to the doctor but there is only a detached condescending stare the doctor knows the man is a schizophrenic he knows that the man does not perceive himself in a rational manner it is sometimes said that people who suffer from schizophrenia have formed an invisible bond with other levels of being that they are the ones who truly see and know what is happening that what we believe to be normal and sane is the illusion the man asks the doctor repeatedly *why am I asked if I believe in God? why am I asked how many times a day I use the toilet? this is harming me!* but his release interview does not go well he becomes agitated and soon the attendants stop him and with a firm grip escort him out of the room the doctor smiles he laughs knowingly as he lights a cigarette he speaks to his colleagues sitting at the table he says this man exhibits the classic symptoms of a schizophrenic he feels persecuted he thinks we are trying to harm him he does not understand why he is here he does not understand

*

The delusions reached the point where she became hostile, even violent. It was heartbreaking for her parents to see their little girl slowly transform into a vicious animal. Sometimes the psychotropic medications would reach her, would help to restore some of her rational mind. But that was short lived. The doctors explained that this kind of deep psychosis, often manifesting itself in cases of schizophrenia, is like an emotional shape-shifter. There would be times when their daughter regained enough of her powers of reason and perception to allow her to negotiate with everyday reality in a normal way. There is no way to predict what results could be achieved until each of the medication combinations were tested. Frankly, the doctors confessed, this was a crap shoot, a hit or miss process. Nothing was guaranteed. The princess wanted her father to be fair minded and to let the prince decide where the wedding was to be held. This did not sit well with the King. After all, the princess was his daughter, and he held dominion over the lands. Why should the prince's family be allowed to make decisions about the wedding? Why should her doctors make independent decisions about the shock treatments? Her mother could not accept the severity of her daughter's mental deterioration.

*

"I don't want to eat my dinner now, mommy! I'm writing my wedding invitations!"

"You can do that later sweetie. Your food is getting cold."

"Stop the shock treatments! Leave her alone! This is destroying her!"

"There are times when the shock treatment coupled with medication can have positive results."

"I don't care! You can't force me to eat when I don't want to!"

"Don't speak to me like that young lady! You come in here and have dinner!"

"I am the princess! I will have you taken to the dungeon! Guards! Guards!"

"But why does she become so agitated and violent?"

"We don't really know. Sometimes patients suffering from acute schizophrenia exhibit a tendency towards violence and aggression, especially when they are younger."

"The more I listen to all of you, the less convinced I am that anyone knows what is really going on with my child!"

"Honey, don't accuse them like that, they're only trying to—"

*

it is an inhuman cry it is as though wild animals have been caught and are being dragged away from their homes they know they will never return instinctually they know so they weep and cry and tear and bite against the metal nets but it is useless the nets are made of knotted steel loops and links so the crying is useless the animals know they are being taken away and nothing can stop it just like these bodies of humans emptied of their souls and the content of their lives spilled across the filthy tile floor of their rooms it is one final cry in which rebellion and defeat coexist like the animals there is the recognition that nothing will save them so there is this hauntingly desperate attempt to make it stop to escape but there is no stopping there is no escaping that's what they say that you can hear them screaming every night all night yes it is all

through the night as if they take turns first it's the ones in the violent ward then it's the ones in the manic ward there is an old man who used to be a teacher every night he thinks he is a little boy he asks his mother to forgive him for making such a mess in his room will she please give him another chance he promises to be good he promises the faceless pillow on his bed that has become his mother's face he pulled out tufts of his hair and made them stick to the pillow with saliva it is his mother she has just come back from the beauty parlor she has a new hairdo she is upset with him because he made such a mess in his room he begs the pillow to forgive him he weeps when he gets no reply he knows that means his mother does not forgive him he will have to be punished he knows what that means he is afraid he tries to hide by covering his face with his hands he thinks this way his mother cannot find him but she will find him she will put him in the closet that is his punishment he must learn his lesson the closet is so dark and so cold a thin shaft of light seeps in through the door crack he can see very little the light makes shadows inside the closet he can just barely make out a few of the buttons on his mother's dress but he cannot stop his thoughts he thinks the little buttons are the beach balls that his father brought to the shore that they played with on the beach then the buttons become howling clown faces they laugh at him they are cruel in their mockery of his plight they know he was not forgiven they know he is a bad boy he must be punished and yet sometimes the buttons become the little glistening Christmas balls on the tree they are reflective and bright he sees himself in their shiny silver reflection he sees himself sitting on his mother's lap he sees himself without pain he sees himself this is the future of the girl with the cape the young girl who wants to be a princess the years will pass there will be no improvement the periods of rationality will become shorter and shorter nothing will prevent the growth of insanity decades will pass her parents will grow old and die hoping that her mind will somehow reconstruct itself she too will grow old long past the death of her parents she too will become an old woman hopelessly insane constantly making capes out of her soiled bed sheets always preparing for her wedding to the prince never understanding what has really happened never seeing where she really is her eyes are like thick lead orbs that cannot be penetrated by x-rays the world in front of her does not exist she does not see what is really there she sees only the endlessly repeating fabrications she's been conjuring since she was a child

*

"So, did you do anything interesting at the coronation today? Did you have any special visitors from far away lands?"

"Oh yes, Mommy! The Duke of Madrid was here for the coronation! He was so very nice! And then I had tea with the Duchess of York! She is so very beautiful!"

"Well, it sounds like you had a very busy afternoon!"

"Oh yes, Mommy! It's so wonderful to be the princess!"

"Do you have anything important for tomorrow?"

"Oh yes, Mommy! Tomorrow is the grand ball! I have to pick out my gown now!"

"Being the princess, you must have dozens of gowns and dresses to look through!"

"Oh yes, Mommy! My attendants will bring them in for me!"

*

nothing is like that subterranean isolation nothing is like that separation from ordinary life screaming every night all through the night as if they take turns first it's the ones before shock treatment then it's the ones after shock treatment towards morning it's the gentle sobbing as if they know as if within the silent shafts of morning sun there is some kind of intuitive recognition of what happened to them as if there was a coded communication between members of a secret society they seem to know they seem to weep for what they used to be what they are no longer there is a sadness beyond the measurable content of language it is said that nurses who look after terminal patients in their final hours often see a last tear roll down the cheek of the dying a farewell to what was a goodbye to the body that is no longer healthy a profound moment of being separated from that which is no longer useful to them it could be that those who scream at night and sob in the morning have made a similar discovery they realize sanity is no longer part of the mechanics of their minds as if they awoke from a terrible accident to discover that they have become quadriplegics they no longer belong in the world of limbs and mobility

*

It is a sacred coronation. Attendants are bringing her the scepter. The Duke of Madrid is smiling at her. He is quite smitten. There is talk in the kingdom that he will be invited to the ball. Will he and the princess marry?

*

"Oh yes, Mommy! I want to marry him! He is so handsome!"

"Yes he is! Well, I have to start dinner now. Maybe you can invite the Duke?"

"That's a wonderful idea, Mommy! But I have to send for my messenger. He'll have to get his horse ready so he can make the journey to the Duke with my invitation."

"Maybe you should write it now so you can give it to the messenger before we have dinner."

"Good! I'll do it now, Mommy."

"Please come back to us, my lost precious daughter...Please be who you were."

"You're not my mother! You are a traitor! A spy from France! You came here to poison me, I know all about it! Guards, guards!"

"Give her another dose of Thorazine."

"Doctor, what good does this do? Why can't we help her become herself again?"

"I'm afraid that these schizophrenic episodes will become longer and more intense. The medications we've been trying haven't had much impact. It's the luck of the draw, I'm afraid. With cases of schizophrenia, you try different combinations of meds and hope you hit the right group that will resurrect some of the patient's normal self. But in your daughter's case, I'm afraid that her psychosis is too far gone."

"Mommy! Mommy! My messenger just returned with wonderful news!"

"I'm in the kitchen, sweetheart. What did the messenger say?"

"He said the Duke would be delighted to attend!"

"That's wonderful!"

"I must tell the tailors to fashion me a new cape, something marvelous!"

"Yes, that would be very special!"

"It should be maroon velvet with gold embroidery, right mother?"

"That's a perfect idea! And with a hood of course, right?"

"Get her other arm, strap her in!"

"I'm trying to get the mouthpiece ready!"

"I thought they stopped shock treatments for this one?"

"They're trying a new med, they think it will help."

"Guards! Guards! These ruffians are assaulting me! Guards!"

"She never stops with the princess thing, does she?"

"Oh, that's a lovely idea, mommy! A hood!"

"Yes, and with a bonnet back, you know, you've seen those."

"Yes, mommy! That sounds wonderful!"

*

Not a princess demons dance schizophrenic Hell all thinking fiery monster puzzles. Beyond reason struggle dance edges against spirit. Endless torment glass shattering skull holds confused weapons attack. Lofty dreams little girl another time another dimension that way that being ended. Cold gel electrodes temples attacked current. Convulsions bubbling saliva not the coronation not that way. Yearning misery unable unwilling vexation no longer childhood all magic gone. Sorrow shadows winding not the happy contours of childhood. Lost never to be repeating laughter all deformed. Rebellion of objects. Rebellion of time. Nothing will quiet the agony of not being what one was. Inner tumult beyond words beyond reason how can it be she is not the princess. Like the explosion of bells lifted into new chaos each day not a shred of what was. Life lifted onto slaughter tables long marble tables ready like ancient Druid sacrifice altars. Wind of sanity not full only tortured zephyrs weep. Taken away smell of alcohol smell of her screams twisting knots of bed sheets not her cape attendants take her. Such a sorrow all deformity of mind morbid transformations of spirit always this remorse.

*

That's what they say. No longer childhood.

All magic gone.

The Imposter

Mu

"no," "not," "nothing," "without," "nothingness," "is not," "has not"

Modern Chinese, Japanese, Korean

MU HAD FINALLY grown weary of running from his sorrow. His entire life had been a tapestry of shadows, a matrix of hypnotic boxes, a sea of spirit traps. He realized that his hundreds of little Internet videos, on Cyber Diary, *formed an imaginary bridge, a way of falsely transferring himself across an abyss of remorse and hopelessness. How much longer could he pretend? Until now, his words repelled the truth. It was as if the very air that shaped the sentences in his mouth was the invisible resistance that compelled two magnets to repel one another and truth was in the center of that repulsion. Mu videoed what he knew would be his last words, hoping that speaking the truth might bring him some salvation before he ended his life. Where was the woman he convinced himself was in his life every day and night?* She never became a woman. *Mu finally uttered the unutterable in front of the humming video camera. He shuddered as he spoke the heartbreaking words, his hand twitching dramatically like a divining rod pointing in the direction of underground minerals. "She died at the hospital. She was fourteen," he said to the staring black instrument that, on this final, fateful evening, acted as a faceless confessor, a way for Mu to admit to himself that* everything *had been a fantasy. He checked the revolver to be sure the chamber was full; then he made what would be the last entry in his video diary: "The real imposter was my phantasmagoric wife, my conjured life that I invented so I could escape the reality of being responsible for a horrible thing. I ate peanuts and forgot about her allergy. I kissed my beloved at the movies and she died shortly afterwards. I loved her so! My sweet Juliet." Even though she was only fourteen and Mu barely more than sixteen, it was an intuition of soul mate destiny felt and certified only in the hearts of those who know it. "After her death," Mu continued, "I used my videos to create in words and images what the years of our evolving lives might have been." Mu turned his video diaries into the life that this tragic accident had taken from him. He was always fascinated by the mechanics of video and film, the neuroscience of sound and image reproduction. His father frequently bought him small, primitive video recorders and 8mm cameras; he spent countless hours filming and playing back anything that crossed his path in a normal day: traffic, footsteps, dogs barking, his parents talking, television commercials. No wonder that his tragic, life-long obsession with creating an illusory world of words and images was so easily facilitated by his desire to make a visual record of the world he knew. The Internet, with websites such as* Cyber Diary, *enabled Mu to upload and maintain hundreds and hundreds of these self-reflexive visual narratives, lasting several seconds to several minutes each. It was unfortunate, ironically, that at the time of the accident, he had chosen the areas of video technology and psychoacoustics for his college study and envisioned future profession. Literally from the day after the death of his girlfriend, until this very moment, Mu lived, if one could use such an extravagant word as "lived," only through his constant, multi-dimensional narrative, in which nothing horrible happened that night at the movies, the girl nestled her head against his shoulder as he drove her home, her hair smelled like jasmine, like aloe, and they were married on the beach, she loved antique furniture, he taught video and cinema history at the university, she gave birth to twin girls, he laughed at the way their boyfriends got confused the night of the prom, his wife made lovely things to eat, he helped with the banana cake mix, she painted by the shore even though her hands shook slightly from a thyroid condition that worsened in her sixties, and the patches of gray in his hair were more visible when he tied it back into the ponytail that his granddaughter compared to Paul Revere (she was studying American history in the second grade). One day, the hellish psychological torment of years of self-imposed subterfuge took their toll. "I began to challenge the authenticity of my self-validated mirage, as if this non-existent lover and companion had been mysteriously substituted by a double or imposter, and the original whisked away into an unknowable dimension, never to be recovered. Instead of allowing myself to realize that the girl in question had died at fourteen, I let her live and grow older, to be in a life with me, through the energy of my videotape entries. The video recordings kept her alive. Just as tragically as Lear realizing far too late that Ophelia was the daughter who truly and selflessly loved him, I came to the realization that my whole life was a myth, a fiction, and I attacked the veracity of what my mind and my voice created, not realizing that I was calling the counterfeit an imitation; that I was rejecting the illusion for being unreal; that I was denying the incantatory for being ethereal." Raising the gun to his temple, Mu finished this final video record of his suicide; he beseeched his loved one to forgive him; and he promised to spend eternity at her side. Mr. Mu stopped speaking for a moment. He pressed the* STOP *button on the video recorder and stared at the table, as if his body and his mind were mysteriously arrested by some kind of trance or hypnotic state. His last thought was that another life in another place seemed to be a fair reward, a special gift after we have atoned for the mistakes we made here. He pressed the* RECORD *button on the camcorder for the last time and spoke: "To be given the chance to love and live again after death, like children reassured after a nightmare, like children eternally playing..." Mu pulled the trigger.*

Hearing the distant church bell, Mr. Mu's doctor set the clock on his mantle and rubbed his sore wrist before lifting the heavy, thick book from the elegant mahogany stand, placing it upon his desk, and turning to the desired page.

Diagnostic and Statistical Manual of Mental Disorders (DSM-5)

The Capgras delusion is classified as a delusional misidentification syndrome, a class of delusional beliefs that involves the misidentification of people, places, or objects. Cases in which patients hold the belief that time has been "warped" or "substituted" have also been reported. It's also known as "Imposter Syndrome." People who experience this syndrome will have an irrational belief that someone they know or recognize has been replaced by an imposter. They may, for example, accuse a spouse of being an imposter of their actual spouse.

"Give her the epinephrine now! Look at the swelling! She can't breathe! She can't breathe!"

"I'm getting the syringe out! We'll be pulling into the emergency room in a minute! The hospital is two blocks away!"

The nervous paramedics moved with an urgency that milked their training and confidence for the precise decisions that were needed but also made their lack of choices all the more desperate. A girl of about fourteen with a dangerously swollen esophagus was about to suffocate as a result of an allergic reaction to peanuts. The syringe with the life-saving drug had to be retrieved from the floor of the ambulance because the sweaty fingers of the attendant let it slip.

Mr. Mu rubbed his tired eyes before lifting the old, dusty, wooden milk crate from the place on the shelf where it rested alongside dozens of identical wooden crates. The decaying, splintered boxes were filled to the top with thousands of neatly, evenly stacked, videocassettes. Sometimes, as on this occasion, Mu liked to watch selections from his immense video library by playing the original tape on the old VHS machine. On most evenings, though, he preferred going to the Cyber Diary *website, where he had previously uploaded the videos, and watch them unfold in myriad waves across the little square screen box on the computer, like an infinite series of undulating spider web compartments.*

These cassettes were stored inside black plastic jackets approximately five inches long. Mu carefully sifted through the top layer of tapes, looking for the most recent date. Many of the tapes in the other crates went all the way back to his teenage years. Finding the one he wanted, Mu pushed it through the slender machine, pressed the "Record" button on the video camera positioned a few feet from his head, and began speaking in a clear voice.

"...let it slip. That was the day that my future wife almost died! All because I insisted on kissing her in the theater before our date was over, even though I had peanuts during the movie and I knew how devastating her allergy could be. It completely escaped my mind! It meant so much to me. After all, I was sixteen and this was our third date! It was time to kiss her; I really liked her! She was so lucky that they had a powerful antidote. They got her to the emergency room on time..."

Suddenly, Mr. Mu, as if exasperated by what he had said, violently rummaged through the crate, moving and disturbing the tapes so ferociously that some of the plastic shells cracked and little loops of videotape spilled out, like curling rivulets of brown blood. It was not clear if he was disgusted by his own account of having been indirectly responsible for causing his young girlfriend's attack and near death, or if he remembered another passage that he recorded previously and wanted to find it as quickly as possible.

"...They may, for example, accuse a spouse..." So you see, Mr. Mu, there is nothing so very alarming here, I mean, in the sense that it has not been diagnostically and statistically examined and encountered many times. Your wife—

—is not my wife. I cannot give you every utterance in my soul that tells me she has been replaced. It would be like the sun asking a lake to prove it deserves to wear the morning on its face. She may reach for a cup; try on a new dress; retrieve a delivered parcel from the front steps. I hear her laughter when something amuses her in the garden; I see her muddied knees after an afternoon of planting. But these are the semblances; some kind of evil incandescence of the one who appears to be her, but is not. It is some kind of sinister metaphysical arrangement, designed long before I was born. A punishment, perhaps, for wrong doing in a past life? I don't know. Some malevolent force has taken away the delicate, sweet creature who came to rescue me from loneliness, and replaced her with a surrogate; as if all madness had stuffed itself into one dark corner of my brain, refusing to leave, removing every hope I might have, every moment I wanted to have, and all the memories I dared to cherish.

"...in a minute! The hospital is two blocks away!"

"Oh God! No! No! She's going into shock!"

Mu's parents continued to provide him with a vast collection of video recorders, plus a steady supply of blank VHS tapes, in spite of the advice from the boy's doctor warning against it. The good will in their hearts blinded their minds to the simple fact that they were enabling the obsessive-compulsive ritual of a traumatized seventeen-year-old boy. A year had passed since the tragedy and the young man continued keeping a videotaped record of it, as though nothing else in his life or his thoughts mattered. He spent every moment of his personal time sitting at his desk filming himself endlessly talking about that day, and then uploading the new entry to the Cyber Diary *website. The doctor's recommendations to get Mu out of the house, to introduce departure from routine or change of scenery, fell on deaf ears. Certainly, his mother and father were alarmed by the morbid accumulation of scrupulously labeled, rectangular plastic tapes in black jackets, yet they felt this was a form of therapy for the boy. They felt that, like an exorcism, the video recordings would eventually free his spirit from the suffocative grasp of negative thoughts and irrational guilt.*

"The parents will be here in a few minutes to bring the girl's clothing and leave a deposit. I'm going downstairs to turn on the lights so they can choose a casket."

"Good. I'll print out the invoice for them. What a shame, huh? Only fourteen. You'd think something like that could have been prevented."

"I heard that the boy she was with—"

"You mean at the movie? Her boyfriend?"

"Her boyfriend, yeah. I heard he really lost it. He's living in a kind of—"

"The psychiatrist? The video tapings?"

"The video tapings, so you heard?"

"My cousin lives near them."

"Near them?"

"Across the street, sweetie. She's such a pretty girl. Why don't you ask her out?"

"Oh mom, c'mon!"

"I'll bet she falls for you! Do you have any classes with her?"

"We're in History, last period."

"Good! There's that new movie—"

"Mom! We haven't even spoken—"

"No one has. His parents are keeping him out of school for now. While he's in therapy and living his life talking to his video cameras. I wonder what that poor girl's parents think of all this?"

"Shh! Here they are!"

This was a special day for Mu. A third date with the girl that he loved so dearly. He wanted to show her that he was serious. After all, he just received his driver's permit and a temporary license! Mu's father was letting him use the family car. "Don't forget," warned his father, "If you scratch the fender, you lose a month's allowance!" Mu promised to be careful and, smiling benevolently, his father's tone softened to warm encouragement as he told his son to enjoy himself. "You're a young man now," his mother added as Mu walked down to the car parked across from the front door, "Are you ready to fall in love?" Mu, a little embarrassed, responded that it was only their third date! They were still in High School, how could they know if they were in love?

Once he was behind the wheel, Mu summoned all the memories he dared to cherish, all the happy thoughts his mind had stored away. Mom must be right, he thought as he drove away. "I must be in love!"

...many times. Your wife, Mr. Mu, is a creature of fantasy, a different and unknown being, only in those secret places of your mind where memory and perception are strangers. How could this woman, who you have known since she was fourteen, how could she not *be the same person? Was she mysteriously replaced by an alien double in the middle of the night? Did some demonic force suck her soul and personality out of her body, leaving only a barren, lifeless shell or mould? Once the mind becomes shipwrecked on some strange island of emotional and spiritual uncanniness, there is little for the conscious part of our brains to do except be carried in tow by our subconscious as it relentlessly explores that island. Are you listening to me?*

"Did you hear me?! She's not breathing!"

"We're here! We're here! Hurry up!"

The frantic paramedics jumped out of the back of the ambulance as it pulled into the entranceway of the emergency room. They banged open the white metal rear doors of the vehicle so forcefully that a violent burst of air made the pair of green movie ticket stubs fly out of Mu's shirt pocket. Frozen in place from shock and the insidious unreality of what was happening, all the poor boy could do was watch the gurney carrying his precious one as it was whisked into glaring hospital lights. He was so terrified. He could not move. He stood there, his arms outstretched, palms facing upward like a supplicant seeking guidance or begging forgiveness. Like a damned sleepwalker on a supernatural path leading towards nothing, radiating outwards in concentric circles of hopelessness, a special kind of subterranean hopelessness designed, like the ninth circle of Hell, only for him. He could not measure the weight of endless shame and guilt that had settled upon the center of his spine. He could not comprehend how he had forgotten about the lethal danger of her allergy. Someone in a car parked a few feet behind him had just turned on the radio and a commercial for tropical vacations came blasting out of the car stereo. The sound of crashing waves overwhelmed Mu with a sense of entrapment, as though he were being swallowed by sonorous enclosure, surrounded by miles of walls of water, buried in an avalanche of suffocation. Maybe this is a nightmare, he thought. Mu wondered: if he concentrated hard enough, if he could palpably and realistically transport himself back to the movie theater, just before he leaned over to kiss her, that maybe the insanity of what had really happened could be somehow transformed or rolled back like a rug being taken out of a room and moved to a new house. There was a truck engine backfiring in rapid staccato bursts: he heard the repeated, failed attempts of the defibrillator. They could not revive her heart. There was a bar across the street with the door open and the third quarter buzzer of the basketball game rang out in a long, linear monotone: he saw the flat line of the droning heart monitor. They could not bring her back. There were dozens of bundles of roses, tight bundles of roses all around her coffin. There were so many times when I thought we laughed. We grew older. She became my wife. It was such a beautiful house! She loved pastels. She wanted Art Deco furniture. I was saving for a surprise on her birthday. A beautiful bar from the 1930s. Lovely marquetry inlay with woods from exotic places. A feast of complexions of wood. Imbedded beautiful layers that shined like an aurora borealis, a kaleidoscopic glow of polished wood. Remember? You were so surprised! So pleased! You hugged and kissed me so many times I began to feel faint with joy. They didn't want me to go to the funeral. My parents were afraid for me. Especially because they had heard that her mother passed out several times; there was talk of her father waiting for me with his gun at the entrance to the funeral home but that turned out to be a rumor. It felt strange seeing so many familiar faces in such an unexpected, unusual place. Students from my math class smoking outside; classmates from Geometry in the front, waiting to kneel at the coffin and pay their respects. We made a home! She didn't die like that. They got her to the hospital in time. The paramedics were ready. They gave her the shot in the ambulance. We made a home! We were so happy. Long walks on the beach at sunset. Listening to the intimate echoes of large shells. Running with the dogs along the shore. Looking at the rows of caskets was too much for the dead girl's mother. She ran up the stairs, sobbing hysterically. It must have been horrific to be so brutally confronted with the death of her daughter. Realizing that she was going into shock, I ran madly into the movie theater lobby to tell someone to call an ambulance. I collided with a man who had just purchased a large container of popcorn. He lost his balance and spilled the yellow puffs all around my feet. They glistened with liquefied butter that created a reflective cluster. I must have remained in that spot, immobilized by fear, because I remember seeing the black wheels of the ambulance stretcher reflected on the oily shine of the popcorn garlands as the paramedics whisked past me. Someone asked Mu if he was with the girl. All he could do was feebly nod his head, still staring at the constellation of scattered popcorn pieces. The theatre manager or a security guard (Mu could not remember) grabbed his arm and quickly ushered him outside so that he could get into the ambulance and ride to the hospital. Mu tried to compose himself and focus his thoughts on how he might be able to help. He asked himself what he knew about his girlfriend's allergy; what useful information could he share with the paramedics. Many teenagers enjoyed group viewings of Cyber Diary *and Mu's videos had become very popular since his girlfriend's death. "I don't want you looking at that boy's videos anymore! It's sick! He talks about that girl as if she's still alive," warned the concerned parent. "Oh mom...We all do! We log on and usually ten of us are looking at the same time. It's really cool! Mu has like hundreds of little videos up there and we put them on our screens ten at a time." A bizarre cult had formed around the morbid ritual of students from Mu's school gathering separately and in unison to watch the videos Mu created in which he seemed to slip deeper and deeper into the psychosis of believing that years were passing and he was having a mature life with his girlfriend. For most of the parents, this became a forbidden form of entertainment, akin to using a Ouija board or experimenting with drugs, forcing the teenagers to arrange more and more clandestine viewings of the website.*

They could not revive her heart. He saw the flat line of the droning heart monitor. Across from the emergency room cubicle, into which the paramedics had wheeled the gurney, an old man was sitting in his soiled hospital gown, holding a little portable radio. A rush of cheering shouts, in bursts and crackles of static, emanated from the little black instrument on the old man's lap. Under the deadly weight of guilt-ridden thoughts that was enveloping and crushing Mu's conscience, his mind was assaulted by a final stabbing irony: these choruses of frantic approval belonged to spectators at the basketball game that, if not for the movie tickets Mu had already purchased, he and his girlfriend would have attended. It was the girl's father who had invited them. He never missed a home game and he would have been sitting courtside with Mu and the girl (he always made sure he procured excellent seats). Racing, pathetically helpless thoughts made Mu imagine that the girl's father was standing with the crowd, shouting for his team, but that he could somehow see what was happening to his daughter in the hospital, because of Mu's carelessness, and his gleeful yelling about a sports victory was nightmarishly and surrealistically combined with a wide-eyed stare, the fixed, terrifying, zombie-like stare of a madman, a stare centered directly and solely upon Mu.

"Hurry up! Let's get inside! There's no pulse!"

"I heard you! I heard you! Open the door! Help me!"

"Get the stretcher ready! The wheels are still locked!"

"Let's get inside! C'mon! C'mon!"

So let's get inside the caves on this unknown island of the subconscious mind. Let's try to see that the thoughts we distrust the most are usually our pathway to mental health, while the thoughts we wholeheartedly embrace often lead to emotion and psychological chaos. I have never met your wife but when you explain that you have known her since your early teens, I must rely on empirical reality, as a doctor and as a rational being, and come to the only plausible conclusion: she must therefore be who she is. She has always been who you say she is. I'm sure you have repeated this to yourself many times.

"How could I think of this as anything but a special day?" Mu's racing, excited thoughts engulfed his mind and controlled his actions.

Yet this was only his third date with the girl! Did he love her dearly? Was he really a serious young man? Mu wondered how he could prove his sincerity. "Don't forget this!" said Mu's father, playfully handing his son the driver's permit that the boy had so eagerly awaited. "A temporary license!" exclaimed Mu just a few hours ago, when he discovered that the long-awaited document had arrived in the mail. Wanting to help his son to relax, Mu's father, in a mock serious tone, admonished him to return the car in perfect condition or he would lose driving privileges for six months. Seeing that Mu was chagrined by these remarks, his father quickly added that he was confident of Mu's driving skill and encouraged the boy to have a good time. Mu realized, with surprising maturity, that he was still young a man. He wondered if he was ready to fall in love. "Why should I be embarrassed by all the memories?" Mu asked himself. Mu decided that with so many happy thoughts, he must be in love. He must be ready.

"So does your cousin ever see the guy, the kid I mean, Mu?"

"No, I don't think so. Nobody does, I mean not since it happened. He never comes out. Stays in his room all the time making those little videos that he uploads to *Cyber Diary*."

"Will you keep your voices down! The girl's parents are here and we have to show them the caskets. I think I heard the mother crying. This is the beginning of the hardest things for parents and relatives to do, picking the casket I mean, and clothes for the deceased, flowers, things like that. It's when the reality of it really hits home. Very hard to watch."

"Sorry. Do you think they'll want to see wood or metal?"

"Not sure. Just let them look at everything down there. Maybe only the father will go. I can still hear the mother. She doesn't sound too good."

"We have some of the smelling salts here just in case, right?"

"Yes, in that drawer over there."

"What are they, by the way? I've always wondered exactly what's in them."

"Ammonia mainly."

"Did you say Ammonia?" The funeral assistant didn't hear the man properly because of the news station on the radio they brought with them and some resounding church bells from a few blocks away. "Really penetrates when someone faints?"

"Always does the trick."

Mu's parents wanted to pay their respects and go to the girl's funeral. They felt it was the right thing to do. Mu's mother suggested it, as she was somewhat friendly with the girl's mother (they had gone to college together). Mu's psychiatrist thought it might be cathartic for them but recommended that Mu not attend. He wasn't pleased that they continued to provide Mu with a vast collection of video recorders. The steady supply of blank VHS tapes alarmed the doctor when he stopped by to have occasional therapy sessions with Mu. In spite of his advice, the good will in the parents' hearts blinded their minds to the simple fact that they were enabling the obsessive-compulsive ritual of a traumatized seventeen-year-old boy. Hadn't a year passed since the tragedy? Yet the young man continued keeping a videotaped record of it. There was no way to dissuade Mu from thinking and behaving as though nothing else in his life or his thoughts mattered. "He spends every moment of his personal time sitting at his desk, filming himself endlessly talking about that day, and then uploading the new entry to the Cyber Diary *website," wrote the doctor in his therapy journal after one of his conversations with Mu. It was extremely frustrating that the doctor's recommendations to get Mu out of the house, to introduce departure from routine or change of scenery, fell on deaf ears.* Weren't his mother and father alarmed by the morbid accumulation of scrupulously labeled, rectangular plastic tapes in black jackets? *thought the doctor. Somehow they felt this was the most effective form of therapy for the boy. They believed that the video recordings would eventually free his spirit from the suffocative grasp of negative thoughts and irrational guilt, like some kind of emotional exorcism. No matter what he said, the doctor could not dislodge Mu's parents' from this belief.*

"...blocks away!"

"...shock!"

"She's turning white! She's turning white!"

"Give her the shot! Give her the shot!"

First you tell me that I created all of this in my mind because my girlfriend died from the trace of a peanut butter sandwich on my saliva, then you say my wife is obviously a real person because she could never have been replaced. Yet every utterance in my soul tells me she has been replaced. I cannot give you proof because the certainty resides within me. "Try a little mental exercise, like imagining the sun asking a lake to prove it deserves to wear the morning on its face." Mu laughed at the doctor's ridiculous attempt to make a metaphorical or poetic suggestion. He explained that his wife was such a clever non-entity, that she knew how to invisibly transit between the real and the unreal. He explained that she might reach for a cup; try on a new dress; retrieve a delivered parcel from the front steps. "I hear her laughter when something amuses her in the garden," Mu explained. "I see her muddied knees after an afternoon of planting." "These are not semblances!" exclaimed the psychiatrist, raising his voice and deliberately adopting an authoritative tone. Sometimes a sudden change in demeanor can challenge or shock a patient and force them to confront their own subterfuge and self-deceit. Mu knew the secret. He knew this was some kind of evil incandescence of the one who appears to be her, but is not. Or maybe it was some kind of sinister metaphysical arrangement, designed long before he was born? "A punishment, perhaps, for wrong doing in a past life? Like the little girl that wasn't ready to be born? Jung." The doctor hurriedly scribbled these notes into his black leather journal. I don't know. *Mu's thoughts echoed what the doctor wrote.* Some malevolent force has taken away the delicate, sweet creature that came to rescue me from loneliness. I recreated her so perfectly. Can't you see? *The doctor glanced at his appointment book and realized that Mu's time was almost up. He had skipped lunch and was famished. There was a new Thai restaurant across the street that he wanted to try.* We came home together from the movie theater that night. We continued dating. We went to college at the same time. *"His guilt layers are so dense and strong," wrote the Doctor in a scribbled handwriting. He had become jittery with hunger. "I'm not having any success penetrating these layers. He will not remember what really happened that night at the movies. His girlfriend died that night."* Why was she replaced with a surrogate? It was as if all the madness of the universe had stuffed itself into one dark corner of my brain, refusing to leave, removing every hope I might have, every moment I wanted to have, and all the memories I dared to cherish.

"...accuse a spouse." Mu's father slowly closed the psychiatric manual with an attitude of morbid resignation. He shook his head sorrowfully, in pitiful recognition of his son's tragic fate. He could already see the life of his son, continuing to shrivel and die within these imagined scenarios that he videotaped every day, then uploaded to the Cyber Diary *website each evening. He envisioned the hundreds of conversations that would occur between his young son and his later self, preserved like an electronic ghost on these videos. With great sorrow, he saw his son, grown into a pathetically confused mature man, a man who had remained so imprisoned and poisoned by his own mental cages, he could never be at peace, even if he were to find a woman to marry. Mu's father could not*

hear or see a future world for his son that was not contaminated by the boy's contorted, infected, insane belief that his girlfriend (who had died purely by accident because Mu had forgotten about her peanut allergy) had in fact lived, that she and Mu married, had children, and enjoyed a long, productive life together. As Mu's psychiatrist had prophetically warned long ago, the fantasy eventually turned in on itself, and Mu began to believe that his wife (who did not exist in the first place) had somehow become an "imposter," a malevolent doppelganger, determined to destroy his soul.

Mu remembered so many things; too many things. He remembered another passage that he recorded previously. Suddenly, he wanted to find it as quickly as possible, as though it held the answer to one of the special secrets that slowly burrowed into Mu's mind every moment of his life. "That's ridiculous!" Mu said out loud. He was exasperated by these thoughts. Speaking to himself, just like the thousands of short videos, was his way of creating and preserving a dialogue with his soul. So he rummaged through the crate more and more violently, like a gasping man on some prehistoric planet clawing at old materials trying to find an oxygen mask. He dug into the tapes, smashing and flinging them ferociously. Cracked shards of the plastic containers, the "shells" that held the videotape, flew into his face. Fortunately, this explosion of sharp pieces did not cut Mu's skin. The loosened tape spiraled out, like rivulets of flowing brown blood. What could have upset him so much? It might have been one of his earliest videotape diaries. During that period, Mu was vehemently disgusted by the realization that he had nearly caused his girlfriend's death. It was the tyrannical combination of desperation and fear that filled Mu with so much rage. His utter stupidity almost cost this girl her life, the person that Mu, carried away by the ardent fantasies of youth, had hoped to marry. In one day, several months after the accident at the movie theater, Mu consecutively uploaded fifty videos to the *Cyber Diary* website. He liked doing it that way, as opposed to saying everything he wanted in a single videotaping and then loading the solitary video. There were no time restrictions. *Cyber Diary* allowed its mostly teenage users to pontificate, rant, and rave all they wanted. The only rule or restriction was that each video entry had to have a kind of "slate" at the beginning and the end, the way the familiar black and white clap board is used in films to mark a new scene with both an aural and visual cue. It was so that the *Cyber Diary* audience could become more intimately familiar with those "Cyber D's," as they were called, that they liked the most, and it also served as a kind of branding or host identification, with each person saying who they were and engaging in a little small talk, at the beginning and the ending of the entry. Letting it slip, failing to include these little bits of personal business, could cause a suspension of use for the "Cyber D" who ignored the procedures of the site.

"...we went over this so many times, man! We trained! Oh God! Got her pulse!"

"...sorry! What do you want?! I got nervous! My hands are sweating!"

"What if she dies!? What if she dies!?"

"Here! Here it is! Got the syringe now!"

This could have been a terrible shame, an unforeseen, monstrous tragedy. Yet somehow, miraculously, they got her to the emergency room on time. This could have been one of those cases where an allergic reaction was as deadly as a bullet to the heart.

I hope he kisses me! He's so cute. It's our third date! I really like him!

"...he must be an idiot to forget a thing like that! Peanuts!"

"...a faint pulse! OK! OK!"

"She's lucky we had the right antidote!"

After lifting the coffee mug to his lips, the detective continued typing the report about the girl who died from an allergic reaction.

He felt sorry for Mu's father. He rubbed his red, tired eyes before inserting another form into the old, dusty typewriter. The precinct was being slowly outfitted with a new communications and computer system. The ancient Royal *typewriters were all that could be set up for now. On the floor next to the officer's desk was a crate taken from its place on a shelf in the Mu home, where it rested alongside one or two identical wooden crates. The new, smooth, blond wood had a pleasant smell, like freshly cut pine. The crates contained a few videocassettes used in early* SONY *camcorders that were bulky and somewhat difficult to operate. The detective asked Mu's father if his son had used the video camera on many occasions. He said that Mu liked to watch selections from the immense video library at the university he attended. He played many original tapes by current and previous students on the old VHS machines. Mu was just beginning to explore the technology and hadn't shot many of his own tapes yet. He had begun to familiarize himself with the* Cyber Diary *website and spent most evenings at home exploring it. The detective had heard of the website and Mu's father explained that from what he had gathered, it was extremely popular with high school and college students. It was a forum for the students to upload their videos that featured all sorts of biographical content: their hobbies; their romantic exploits and conflicts; their taste in music and clothes; academic interests, career plans, and so forth. "It's like an infinite series of undulating spider web compartments!" was the elegiac explanation Mu once tried to articulate to his father, attempting to justify spending countless hours sitting in front of his computer, watching hundreds if not thousands of these videos unfold like myriad waves across what appeared to Mu's father to be a little square screen box. "That's the* Windows Media Player, *dad!" Mu explained.*

On the day the detective retired, several piles of case notes had been made available to him. He was given special treatment at the precinct because he was well liked and had spent thirty-five years on the force. The "Mu" case was special to him because even though he never revealed personal information to Mu's father at the time that he typed the report, he was especially touched by what happened to Mu's girlfriend because he and the girl's father had been friends for many years. Of course, once the circumstances surrounding the girl's death were determined to be accidental, and the case was officially closed, the detective filed his notes and moved on. Now, all these years later, he wondered about Mu the middle-aged man, still living in his parents' house, and, from gossip that occasionally made its way into the precinct, still obsessed by the same demons, the same videocassettes. The detective finished his report, typing that these cassettes were stored inside black plastic jackets approximately five inches long. Mu carefully sifted through the top layer of tapes, looking for the most recent date. Many of the tapes in the other crates went all the way back to his teenage years. Finding the one he wanted, Mu pushed it through the slender machine, pressed the "Record" button on the video camera positioned a few feet from his head, and began speaking in a clear voice, looking directly into the camera.

It took many years of psychotherapy for the young paramedic to rid himself of his irrational guilt. He tormented himself with the unshakable belief that the girl died only because his slippery grasp of the syringe caused it to fall to the ambulance floor. He retrieved it almost instantly yet it was impossible for anyone to convince him that those additional two or three seconds meant nothing and could not have saved the girl from death. For the unfortunate young man, these seconds might as well have been days. He was so overcome with grief that he tried to take his own life on several occasions. He would have been successful had it not been for the watchful eyes of his parents. Fortunately, after more than a decade, and the sensitive support of his mother and father, he began to see the event through an objective lens that revealed his blamelessness, rather than the expressionistic vision of his imagined guilt and incompetence that had been tormenting him for years.

"Why isn't she breathing yet?! She's not breathing! Isn't the epinephrine working?! What happened?! What happened?!

"Look! We're pulling into the emergency room now! I just gave her the shot!"

"I thought you lost the syringe! What were you doing on your hands and knees just now?! Did you drop it?! You're sure you gave her the shot, right?!"

"Yes, yes! I gave her the shot!"

Cases in which patients hold the belief that time has been "warped" or "substituted" have also been reported. Patients suffering from this affliction do not experience time as a linear companion. Instead, they are often terrorized by what appears to be the malignant intrusion of time, as though it did not belong where it insinuated itself, as though it attacked instances of being or memory with irrational and contradictory elements, elements that did not make logical sense, leaving the patient in a kind of kaleidoscopic daze, a jumbled landscape of illusory, ill-fitting, sardonic parts, not the pleasantly discordant parts of a fantastical dream, but the monstrously mismatched parts of a hideous nightmare.

Mr. Mu's doctor only worsened the arthritic symptoms he had been feeling in his wrist by slamming the gargantuan psychiatric tome shut with all the force of disgust he could muster. Such elegant descriptions! *he thought, hating the impotence he felt over his inability to reach Mu and help him see reality.*

"Did you hear that?"

"What? I don't know. C'mon, it's your turn."

"It sounded like a gun shot. Didn't you hear?"

"Yeah, so? Maybe a car backfired. C'mon."

"We'll get our Easter dresses dirty. My mom will kill me."

"It's just a little Hopscotch, silly."

"All right. All right. But we're stopping as soon as mass begins."

"You had to jinx us. There go the bells!"

"Let's get inside! It's Easter mass!"

"I never stood so close to a church on Easter Sunday before! The bells are so beautiful!"

"They are wonderful! So many, too! But so loud! I can barely hear you!"

"I can barely hear you too! Sister at school says the Easter bells tell everyone that the fasting is over!"

"Right! Because Christ has risen!"

"Right, the Resurrection! The chance to live again after death! Let's get inside!"

"Let's get inside!"

Bong! BongBong! BongBong! Bong!

BongBongBong!

BongBongBong!

Bong! BongBong! BongBong! Bong!

Burial

Leaves and twigs scattered suddenly, as if the last, hurried pat of her seven year old palm, hitting the flattened surface of moist earth that moments ago revealed a fourth hole, was somehow acknowledged by the secret watchfulness of nature, and the little whisking breezes, surrounding her finished labors, had somehow bestowed their blessing upon her task.

She had left the house as surreptitiously as her tiny form and sincere energy would allow, running down the old boards, almost jumping across the eighteenth century backdoor steps of the farmhouse, charging into the woods like an infantryman rushing into battle, head held high with quiet dignity and deadly purpose, without even an atom of fear, soul impervious to danger, defying threats to life and limb, lying just ahead in the enemy's midst.

She felt that if the subjects of her special mission showed great strength and courage, then so should she, therefore she looked upon her four inanimate playmates with a mixture of wonder and resignation, and so, the night before at bedtime, she watched them reverently as they sat in a Buddha pose, exhibiting an air of perfect composure, their faces cradled by the soft glow of moonlight, their eyes looking straight ahead with resolve and confidence.

*It would not be a communal grave; she wanted above all for each of her sweet friends to be laid to rest in his or her own sacred plot, so that the dog (*Snowflake*), the cat (*Marshmallow*),* Raggedy Ann, *and* Raggedy Andy *were to be given the same privacy and decency one would expect from the funeral of a deceased loved one, as each soft, delicate figure was loved by her, as if it were indeed a family member, and in her young heart, each one had died a kind of spiritual death, not a physical or a biological end,* *but something far worse, and in her young mind, which possessed wisdom far advanced for her age, wisdom that was shamelessly forced to coexist with her innocence, the only way to save the purity of her playmates' existence was to remove them forever from the eyes of the living.*

She knew, of course, that there was a solemn finality to this act; she had considered other means of burial which seemed to offer the same degree of respect but which, unfortunately, lacked the same quiet efficiency as the earth: a stone tied to each of their necks followed by a loud splash in the pond that was too close to the house and therefore presented the risk of unwanted noise and attention; a funeral pyre with the bodies of her friends neatly stacked in a crisscross pattern that, again, would risk discovery either because of smell (the burning figures' clothing and buttons would surely waft into the house, stinging her mother's otherwise unblinking, expressionless eyes) or sight (it would not take long for clouds of thick gray smoke to fill the deep blue sky and be noticed between the bare November branches by her father as he went through the woods deer hunting); no, only the participation of the silent earth, offering its mystery of covered holes as a kind of accomplice, could defeat the tyranny of the senses and negate the influence of sound, smell, and sight.

The ancient instinct in all sentient beings, human or animal, to protect and comfort helpless young, has immeasurable dignity, and perhaps by symbolically adopting this role of the beneficent mother, she somehow restored to her spirit and her psyche a portion of the pure joy and carefree love of life that had been so brutally taken from her.

This joy, this love: the ordinary, commonplace ingredients of the life of a child, were never for her the genuine gifts they should have been; in her world, they were counterfeits, imposters, charlatans and false prophets; their deception came from the lowest rungs of humanity's ladder, and what was most touching about her refusal to give back hate and scorn, but to instead bestow only gentility and kindness upon the world, was the way in which these obscenities, masquerading as offers of goodness, constantly led her to expect love and trust, only to spit at her love, to ridicule her trust, to prove to her again and again that cruelty, depravity, anger and intolerance were the four walls of her prison, and that because she was a child, she could not escape.

There was an immense cornfield down the road, behind her parent's farmhouse; her father would call out to her on summer nights, angrily demanding that she make her way through the towering, moonlit stalks, so radiant and majestic in the musky perfume of July country nights; finally, almost magically safe, she comforted her mind and body as if, for just a few moments, this metaphysical union of spirit and matter belonged only to her, as if her being and her senses functioned first and foremost for her own pleasure, and as if the glow of the diamonds in the black velvet cape of night was intense and pulsated only because of her imminent rescue, that moment of drama, the intervention of the caped hero at the last second, and the all encompassing arms of the night, reaching down to take her away, as she lay on the ground in the middle of the cornfield, looking up at the sparkling ancient sky.

The cornfield had become her sanctuary, her escape; an oasis of fantasy where her imagination ruled and the malignant realities of the farmhouse disappeared; the farther she ventured into the multiplying matrixes of leafy giants, the more she felt the dissolution of her body, and the more she felt the freedom of her senses, the release of all sensate modalities, the miraculous freedom of being allowed to feel and hear, to touch and see and smell what she chose, the way a bird decides where to build its nest, the way a ghost crab delicately emerges from a hole of glassy pebbles, sprightly sidling along a sunset-drenched shore.

She froze suddenly, having filled the last hole in a kneeling position; her father had taken two shots in rapid succession at some bucks; she was familiar with the sound of the high-powered rifle he used for deer when he hunted on his property; momentarily startled and remaining on all fours, she found it strange (even though she had heard these sounds hundreds of times) that the report of the gun always created waves of thrashing and squawking sounds as hundreds of frightened birds flew maniacally off the branches, violently pulling out leaves and twigs in their wake, as if the trees had been pulverized by the winds of an atomic explosion.

Her father's reflection appeared on the shiny, slippery black orb of the dead buck's eye; reaching up to gut the carcass, his undulating, distorted form seemed to loom over the trees, as if he were a giant emerging from some dark, forbidden part of the forest, preparing to devour his kill; at the same instant, she arose, straightening herself, while in a very low voice she uttered prayers intended to guide the souls of her sacrificed brethren to a heavenly plane; but just as the gleaming iris of the slaughtered beast made her father look like a gargantuan, supernatural thing, the square, yellow plastic garnet of her toy ring, in the fierce glare of midday sun, gave her a compressed, shrunken appearance; having dutifully accomplished her honorable task, her heart felt stronger than a thousand oceans, but the illusion of perspective on the surface of the ring made her look no taller than a blade of grass.

It was perfectly natural for the girl's father to dress out a deer or any other game that was in season right at the spot where he made the kill: this saved him the trouble of twice carrying the offal collected in a pail; had he performed the gutting and skinning in his basement, he would have to bring the pail back into the woods, about half a mile from the house; he often left the innards of his kill as well as assorted food garbage from his family just beyond his property as a way of keeping smaller, scavenging creatures such as opossums, raccoons, foxes and so forth from coming too close; everything in his world of hunting was calculated for maximum efficiency: he was a cold, one dimensional, one minded man who did not see a microdot of gray in the world; its inhabitants, its events, and its meanings were strictly and savagely black and white to him.

The cruelest dimensions of his nature manifested themselves primarily through this strictness of viewing, understanding, and judging the world; ownership, especially the primitive rights of those who own, who possess, who wield sovereign power and control over that which belongs to them, these were the only rituals of mind and matter that earned his attention and respect; for him, every conceivable manner or method of ownership (including all abominations of behavior that kowtowed to the lowest instincts of man) reverberated with the echoes of a life well spent, a dedication to Puritan laws of work and God, and a sacrifice of the self in servitude to the needs and welfare of the family.

A curious parallelism of movements occurred: as the girl slowly stood up, during the silence that ensued after the gun's report faded and many of the birds returned to the trees, she relaxed somewhat and slowly took a few steps backwards, smiling at her finished work, at the carefully flattened soil that now concealed four tiny graves, and, just as she backed up a little in this admiring regard of the dirt, her father wiped blood and oily fluids from his hands as he slowly took a few steps backwards as well, contemplating with equal satisfaction his completed task of evisceration, and deciding that the carcass was ready to be brought back to the house (first he would scatter the entrails collected in the large metal bucket).

She did not understand, yet somehow she knew her deeds today held a kind of sacredness, something that could be preserved and revered in her mind and her heart, unsullied by time or circumstance, something that could not be compromised or made foul, the way the dandelions and short grass were deformed just now, buried under the rising steam and bloody slime of the dead creature's insides, her father having dumped the bucket, making all the glistening portions of internal organs scatter about, some of them clinging like rubbery cobwebs to stalks and bushes, most of them unfolded and layered upon the earth, like pink and red lava from a purging volcano, bubbling prehistoric waves of matter, invading and destroying the decorum of nature and civilization.

There was no compassion in the aftermath of this butchery. Her father was performing a functional act by leaving the entrails along the perimeter of his property, just as he would often bring out buckets of discarded food to the same general area. It was bizarre that the severity of his thinking never included an awareness of how these deeds were a form of sustenance for the small creatures that roamed around his land. The fact that these acts kept the animals nourished and alive never entered his mind. She knew this better than anyone. She knew that his only interest was in preventing the scavengers from coming too close to his house, a sealed world that would always remain private and inaccessible to outside scrutiny. There were two reasons he did not simply exterminate the animals: the first was that such a holocaust would disrupt the balance of nature in his hunting zone, eliminating the food supply of the animals he liked to hunt (deer and ducks for example) and eventually driving them away. The second reason was pure inflexible dispassionate practicality: there would be countless trips to collect and dispose of the carcasses. So to think of this distribution of the innards of his kill as a form of humane regard for the raccoons and opossums and foxes would be like thinking that barbed wire is a welcome sign to trespassers because it is not electrified. He was a very successful salesman who possessed a powerful, instinctual understanding of the difference between surface appearance and private content. She and her siblings were never allowed to invite school friends to the house; visiting the homes of their classmates or any other children they knew was forbidden; strangers of any kind were always kept at a distance; on the rare occasions when her father allowed her to receive a doctor's care, he would obstinately and obtrusively hover over the examination, no matter how small or minor the ailment or bruise that necessitated the visit. She would develop a life-long anxiety about fundamental health issues and doctor visits in general as a result of her father's morbid rituals of possessiveness and inappropriate attention when she was examined. Therefore, her emotional education regarding the contradictions and hypocrisy of her father's behavior and habits gave her a critical acumen far beyond the maturity of her years. She knew that he was motivated only by this maniacal need for privacy. He did not care one iota for the welfare of the smaller animals whose existence was supported by his steady supply of offal. If he could have scoured the forest with an automatic weapon and eliminated all of these little beasts without adversely impacting the steady supply of larger prey that he so enjoyed hunting, he would have done so with glee punctuated by a soulless grimace. Of course, all of this was the private content that he was so skillful at concealing. None of his neighbors had the slightest idea that he performed what they saw as humanitarian deeds only for the express purpose of guaranteeing the presence of the other animals that he hunted, killed, and butchered. The final step was the taxidermist so yet another stuffed carcass could be displayed in his "great room" with its forty foot ceiling and walls filled with the mounted motionless bodies of bears, deer, elk, caribou, and others. She knew that an inexhaustible supply of frightening anger always smoldered within him. There was no way to anticipate or prepare for it. She and her siblings knew that he was extremely mercurial and could transition from irrational hostility to goodnatured cheer in a flash. Their only coping mechanism was to determine what mood had taken hold of him for that day and to act accordingly. If he was antagonistic and violent, the only recourse would be to immerse themselves in homework and household chores, to stay out of his way as much as possible. Nevertheless, he would always find some wrong or fault in what they had done, and physical punishment soon followed. If he was pleasant and ebullient, he would encourage them to play and often join in, full of paternal benevolence and happy spontaneity. A classic example of bi-polar personality disorder, although, to his children, there was only the daily torture of not knowing if their father would be loving or hateful, thus depriving them of the precious consistency that is so essential to the emotional evolution and psychological well-being of a child. He felt that the children were his property. He believed he had the right to do whatever he wanted with them. She knew the hunting was over because the rifle fire had subsided. He said goodbye to his hunting buddies and hoisted the disemboweled body onto the wagon he used to bring back heavy game. She gave the burial area a final look and tried her best to clean the dirt from her dress. She knew he would want to know how she got dirty. He shut the meat freezer lid in the garage after depositing the animal. He went into the house and removed his clothing. She walked up the stairs as slowly and quietly as possible. She went into her room and sat on the bed. He followed her and closed the door.

"Your father used *Snowflake* and the others?"

"He put them into sexual positions?"

"Including his penis?"

"He wanted you to think it was innocent play?"

"We don't have to talk about it this week if you don't want to."

"Most of this happened more than forty years ago."

"It takes time."

"I wish I could make the pain go away."

"I know these wounds run very deep."

"So what did you do with all the dolls?"

Unloved

all this shit about it I don't give a shit no more when my man used to get all dressed up for me take me out we just do it back there behind the bar 'cause I was only 15 he didn't want no trouble from it like if I got with a baby and all that and I never had no real fun my daddy made us work in the cotton mill and my hands were always sore I couldn't hardly hear no more from them damn machines like I said I said it already I said it to those police who found him sitting dead on that dock just like I always felt he was going be some kind of trouble to the house just a mouth to feed and a body to clothe and not too smart neither we should have done away with it that night when I squeezed him out and if we lived someplace else that would have been the way too many folks knew I was with a child they could go tell the police and it was just as well he died like he did outside the house so he was beat up yeah I slapped him around some here and there I don't know what's this all about something they said in his brain bled itself to death I wasn't home that night and my man was drunk all right but like I said I just was not there and in the morning the boy was gone so all this shit about it like I said I don't give a shit never wanted that boy anyway and now what's done is done not like he was gonna be no scientist or lawyer or nothing like that the boy was lucky he could count to two an like I says to them social services people it was too much to bear 'cause how was I suppose to give my man all the bedroom time he needed and deserved huh? how I's supposed to take care him and be looking after that child when he almost twelve and got not even the sense of a dog not enough regard for reason come damnation or salvation that boy just had no way out of his sorry head an' I deserves more than a life of caring for a thing ain't hardly human ain't hardly even able to say his name why God make such creatures I just don't know it just can't fathom why the good Lord made that boy just don't know just can't see

****

"Money's no good here tonight, boys. I know it's your job but it must have been Hell taking that poor child's dead body away from the dock, beaten to a pulp and all. So you fellas drink up and don't you worry none about it tonight, you hear?"

"That's a good heart on you, all right, but let us buy you a few rounds back, won't ya?"

"No no no! That's all there is to it now!"

"Can't thank you enough. Much obliged."

"That's right, can't thank you enough. Still don't believe that crazy slut finally let that no good son of a bitch boy friend of hers beat that helpless boy like that, leaving him at the edge of death, and no one no where no how to put a stop to it."

"Shit! We couldn't of saved him if that hospital were just halfway down the road. Been driving an EMS ambulance most of the last twenty years and I never seen anything like this before. How that boy managed to walk two miles to the dock with that much bleeding going on inside his head is just a plain miracle, not that it did him no good, I mean as far as miracles go."

"Yeah, I know it. Me too, I mean I been doing this almost as long as you, never saw a head injury case that bad on a child no more than twelve. Like to know where those goddamn social services people were at all this goddamn time. No reason on earth why that boy shoulda been left in that girl's custody. She never wanted him. Never made no secret of it, neither. Damn system. Just a bunch of offices and forms. Nothing really helps nobody 'cept when they help one another get promotions."

"Yeah, I hear that all right. Poor kid coulda been adopted long time ago."

"Hey...! There's no one to go to the poor kid's funeral! Goddamnit!"

"We'll go! I'll tell you that for sure! Goddammit! We'll go all right! We'll go!"

****

Spppppppppeshul Claasss
Ainngleshh 2

My Storer

Me anz zasun gots a waize taibee wit itsutter. Ma heads aghentz whazever gits whaarrmm. Gits me taibee likesime wit zasun. Weeze bein like weeze wun thang like Ikan go whitever it go like me anz zasun onsa laik ore onsa baks uv dem birz heds. Dems perti soo perti wit dat sun onsa theres winges too likes da waize da morn nin shoostru sphidar weps. Gold morn nin sphidar weps lite.

****

OPERATOR: 911 What is your emergency?

CALLER: (garbled) ...on the dock. Think he's dead.

OPERATOR: Where, sir? You're cutting off. Where are you?

CALLER: Damn it! Over by the bridge, where the dock ends! There's a—

OPERATOR: Route 333?

CALLER: —young boy here...Yeah, Route 333! He's sittin' here all frozen like, seems to be dead. Sittin' on the dock with his head leanin' 'gainst the dock pole.

OPERATOR: Is he breathing? Any sign of a pulse?

CALLER: (exasperated) Well I guess if he's all stiff and frozen in this one position then he must be pretty much dead! I checked his wrist and there ain't no pulse neither.

OPERATOR: So you're over by the dock just under Route 333 with a male child who seems to be dead? Is that right?

CALLER: Yes miss, that is so! That is truly so! Now if you don't mind maybe we can git somebody over t'here so's this poor boy's body can be taken care of proper!

OPERATOR: And there are no vital signs, you say? He appears to be deceased, you say?

CALLER: Yes miss, that is so! I was in the army and I seen my share of combat and I can tell you for sure that this poor boy is stone cold dead!

OPERATOR: Do you know his age or his name or where he lives?

CALLER: Well I can tell you he looks kinda familiar to me but that's about all. I think he's that god-forsaken boy that's not too right in his mind. Lives with that witch of a girl had him so young she weren't more 'an a child herself. Don't know their proper names. She and her man always in trouble always be about abusin' that poor boy. Nobody wanna have much to do wit 'em both 'cept hopin' the authorities might take the boy away some day 'an give him a proper home. Too late fer that now.

OPERATOR: Does the body have any bruises or swelling? Does the boy appear to have been beaten or hit anywhere? I may have to dispatch this as a homicide.

CALLER: (garbled) ...on the head. There's a pretty big gash there. Dried blood all over his neck, shoulders, and his chest, too. He's pretty stiff now and I ain't no medical authority but I can tell from my time in the service that he's probably been dead—

OPERATOR: What, sir? You're cutting off again.

CALLER: —a few hours. I said blood, dried blood! There's lots of dried blood on the head.

OPERATOR: From a blow to the head do you think?

CALLER: I seen enough combat wounds to think so, yes miss, that is so! Looks for sure to me to be a blow to the head. With somethin' sharp, too, cause I can see way into his bone, I can see the space in between the split skull bone.

OPERATOR: All right now sir I'm going to dispatch this call as a possible homicide of a male minor child, already in rigor mortis, dead approximately two hours, presenting a severe head wound, and the body found by you at the dock just under Route 333. Is that right?

CALLER: That is 100% correct Miss. I can't think of anything else. That is 100% correct.

OPERATOR: May I ask you to remain at the scene until the ambulance arrives? It would be helpful.

CALLER: Yes, Miss. I certainly will. I wouldn't think of leaving now. I'm a decent man. Be right here for when them EMS fellas show up.

****

His legs ached and he was still bleeding.

It was not sweat. He could not walk anymore and he sat on the edge of the dock. The blood dripped down across his face and his lips got the metal rust taste of it. His eyes opened and he was still dizzy. He closed them right away. The ocean smelled good. The little waves pounded upon the dock pilings and his body felt their rhythm. He had to rest here. He leaned his head against the railing. The boats looked peaceful. In between the parallel railing bars these four or five sailboats looked like white bar rests on a sheet of music. He kept his eyes closed and enjoyed the womb-like warmth of the sun sunken into the barnacle-laden wood of the dock. He thought of how he tried to make his head join the sun when he was only three or four. On late summer afternoons he would lean his head against something warmed by the sun and with his eyes closed he thought his mind and the sun were doing great things together. They were making forests grow. They were shining on the wrenches of the steelworkers making tall building in cities he had seen only in books. He was shining on the surface of the lake. Snow outside the window could not undo the warmth of his blankets. His shadows stayed up at night telling magical tales of the wonderful things he and the sun had done that day.

The next day they found him sitting in the same position with his head against the dock. Legs crossed and hands folded upon his abdomen, he evoked the classic southern image of a barefoot young boy idling away a summer afternoon fishing, minus the pole, crumpled straw hat, and awkwardly carved wooden pipe.

He bled to death.

****

CUT!

"Wait, the levels were off. Sorry. Could you read it again, just before the end, from 'He was shining'...?"

"You mean from '...on the surface of the lake'...? From there?"

"Yeah that's right. Wait...I have to take this call."

"More Front Office trouble, huh?"

"Shut up! Give me that phone....Hello? Hello?"

"Bet it's about the budget for the 911 call. They used ten cameras."

"Ten?!"

"But we agreed on using all the angles for a more dynamic effect, right? I saw the rushes today. It looks great! And don't forget, like right now we're saving a bundle. Remember, he's doing a voice-over narration, no sets, no production, just him reading it like it was a story being told."

"That was a good idea he had. Cuts out a whole budget day of production work and shooting costs."

"All right. All right. Call you tonight. We'll look at the rushes from today. You'll see. Bye."

"Am I reading this again?"

"Fine. Fine. Just from where I said ...that 'shining' part, OK?"

"Got it."

"OK."

ACTION!

...he was shining on the surface of the lake…

COMPOSITION

The unsteady movement of his slender wrist enables me to hear the remote sounds of a piano. I am usually in another part of the very large house, but at this moment he is just across the hall, writing in the study, describing the piano music.

Occasionally he looks up from the faded, pale notebook paper, gazing through the specially constructed, huge circular window, as if there might be something, an item of scenery perhaps, which might strike his fancy and provide inspiration for his writing. But he knows as well as I that (despite the enormity of the aperture) there is nothing, no landscape, no scenic detail of any kind.

Awkwardly holding the pencil between the thumb and index finger of his right hand, he continues with the work. His hand shakes involuntarily, sometimes to the point where his grasp of the pencil is quite precarious. It may be that this feeling of uncertainty in the act of writing provokes him to go so far as to pretend that the void framed by the window's pane of spotless glass can be filled with a vision of things that are not there.

He is filling the pages with black, crooked letters, slowly writing his description. A thin silver arm (connected to a turntable flanked by two sizable speakers) lightly rests upon a revolving disc. Last night, he stumbled in front of the window, but my guess is that this occurred mainly because he had to pass through many small rooms in order to get to the window, the rooms in which he keeps his paintings of sunsets, seascapes, sprawling mountains, valleys, and the like. And finding this particular record gave him pleasure.

He is comforted also as he makes a comparison between the sides of the pencil and the rooms in the house, realizing that if every side of the pencil corresponded to a room, the number of rooms would far exceed the number of sides, so that (although he may not always be physically in control of the pencil) the rooms are always at his disposal. However, within the darkness of last evening, as he held the record (which I am now playing), he didn't know that I would prefer not to lower the volume of the music. In fact, I vaguely recall that we discussed this record yesterday afternoon, in the bright, peaceful study with the unusually shaped window. During this conversation, he might have assumed that I would not lower the volume, especially when his hand began twitching against his jasmine shirt.

In my obstinance, I must confess that I have been playing this record so loudly that the sound waves emitted from the speakers, creating such a severe impact, have actually produced deep, somewhat oblique cracks in the plastered walls of my distant room. He just completed another paragraph. Here, he refers to the obscure, almost ethereal character of the music. Soon he will grow tired of writing, maybe make a last attempt to trick his mind by looking through the window, relinquish even this distraction, and release the pencil from the tenuous grip of his palsied hand.

The mechanical arm (imperceptibly moving towards the center of the record) remains atop the perpetually turning disc. I have maintained the volume of the music at such a high level for so long a period of time that my senses have become slightly altered or distorted. Perhaps this is too much of an exaggeration. Yet, for one thing, the speakers no longer appear like distinct objects. I cannot truthfully describe their appearance, in fact every aspect of their real dimensions eludes me entirely. For example, their outline (which formerly was quite sharp) has dissolve into a blurry mass, a mass with no periphery. Without any real sense of boundary, I am now unsure of his exact whereabouts, but at least I can move through the house even more freely than before.

He stops writing in the middle of a sentence: now he is trying to conjure an image of the piano on which the piece is being played. The score (which contains the devious black notes of the composition) is placed on a small stand above the keyboard. The pianist strikes the keys quite violently, fully in control of the passage being played, but if this brutal hammering continues, the tumult of vibrations spreading throughout the piano will certainly make the score fall from the stand.

In spite of the rooms filled with paintings through which he passed last night, when he reached the murky study he still couldn't see the window. For that matter, he could barely see his own feet, and he stepped with trepidation, crossing the thick rug which completely muffled his footsteps. Earlier, when we discussed the record, I could see that he was not well: it was easy to observe his pallid complexion, and I realized that the deterioration of his condition was inevitable.

He has just finished writing and he nervously places the pages in the drawer of his desk, anxious as always because of his superstition that the completion of something is a bad omen. There is no solace in having many rooms at his disposal because for the moment the pencil remains inside his breast pocket, and so he is without the original basis for his reassuring comparison. Pieces of cracked paint and plaster may fall onto the desk where these pages have been placed, but it is unlikely that the pages will ever be seen again. Night has fallen, and I can move about with virtually unlimited freedom, although being clumsy I do sometimes falter.

Median

How long he had been there and for what purpose I still cannot say. Even now, after so many years of endless reflection. When one has traveled as far as I, one develops very strict principles, and the strictest of these principles is to keep in motion, to continue the journey at any cost.

But I had stopped and there he was. One does need a momentary respite, even if it is for no other reason than to stand still and look about. He was staring at the pavement, and there his attention was fixed, with a curious intensity which, at the time, immediately struck me as absurd.

This town differed in only one respect from the thousands of towns through which I had already passed: the stones of its pavement were arranged in concentric, ever widening circles. Each ring of stones was circumscribed by another (and naturally larger) ring of stones. And I was not surprised never to have seen such a unique decorative pattern in the towns I previously visited.

Shortly after stopping beside him, he informed me that the circular form of these stones made him unhappy, as if he interpreted my having stopped as a silent inquiry into his state of mind. It is best to remain in motion. The glare of the sun is less aggressive when the body is moving.

Despite my growing annoyance, I somehow found the patience to indulge him and asked with condescension how it could be that the appearance of stones, circular or otherwise, could make a person unhappy. This was his answer: within the very last and smallest circle (which is at the center of the surrounding circles that circumscribe it) is a single stone. This stone, he added, remains different from the others because, unlike them, it is not part of any circumscribing circle, yet it is still circumscribed. Finally, he concluded that this one stone is circumscribed a large number of times, but that even though this unknown number of circumscriptions is certainly quite vast, it is not infinite.

Vast but not infinite! You are a fool, said I. And I continued with the most devastating retort at my disposal, one that I had acquired through my lifelong experience as a traveler, telling him: I suppose you belong to that rare group which maintains that should a person walk straight through the densest and most variously colored forest, then emerge from it to discover the sea strangely laid before one like a carpet before a door, here stand still and look about in any direction one wished, and finally walk quietly into the waves to be convulsively drowned, that such a person would therefore escape the imprisonment of his own end?

Perhaps, he replied, one might see the smooth green peak of a distant mountain while exercising the freedom of looking about in any direction. Then, he added, one could lower one's eyes to the sea and observe its dark green fury, pausing for a moment to look at the waves bursting apart, and shortly thereafter continue walking towards them.

At this point I realized that not only was he an idle fool but that he was also quite mad. I should not have wasted my time with him, or so I thought at that moment. After all, at that stage of my peregrinations, I still had many more towns to see. I left him as I found him, gazing at the rings of stones with an idiotic fixation.

As I was leaving, I turned around and looked at them for the first time. The sun was in its zenith, casting an intense yellow haze upon the innumerable marble stones. The rays glared down upon them, making them glint and sparkle, raising their various colors, mixing and intermingling the shades and hues, so that the stones could no longer be distinguished from one another.

I remember that the sun had set by the time I reached the next town, and so it occurred to me that, now released from the brutal hold of its sharp rays, some of the stones might have regained the solidity and purity of their individual colors.

And now, many wasted years later, having finished my highly informative travels, I vainly try to calm myself with the gentle thought that the single stone in the last circle was not green.

Last Days of Ambrogino

I was told that after the war a patrol of soldiers found me lying unconscious in an abandoned building in a town I could not remember. The soldiers brought me to a hospital where I was gradually revived and given medication for some wounds I had received. These were not gunshot wounds. When I awoke, I could not recall who I was or where I had come from. That is, I did not know if I belonged to this town, or if I had been a soldier myself (I was wearing civilian clothing when they found me). The doctors said that cases of temporary amnesia were common and they had already treated many persons who had experienced it after receiving some kind of head wound. This puzzled me because, as far as I could see and feel, my wounds were on my legs and back. I felt no pain in my head, nor could I feel any bump or gash of any kind. After a few days, I began to feel better. My appetite returned and I enjoyed some meals although the food was very plain and sparse. One evening, a nurse came to me carrying what looked like a ledger book. She sat on a chair next to my bed and explained that this journal was found on my person when I was brought to the hospital on that first day. She wanted me to have it. I thanked her and explained that I still had no idea of who I was and therefore was even more puzzled to discover that I had carried this volume of writings (I assumed that the book had been used and that I was the one who had used it). The nurse explained that my memory would gradually reconstitute itself, that this would be a lengthy process. I thanked her and opened the book. There was indeed a series of writings inside but the words were arranged as a narrative of some kind. I suppose I had expected to see diary entries. Since my own mind was still a tabula rasa to me, I could make no judgment whatsoever about my abilities or tendencies as a writer. I wondered if this could be some kind of military journal. Was I a free-lance writer who had been commissioned to write short stories or political commentary about the war? I found a pen in the little table next to my bed and decided to test whether or not my handwriting matched the penmanship on the pages in front of me. As I copied what appeared to be the title of this work, *Last Days of Ambrogino*, I immediately noticed that my handwriting matched what had been previously written on the front page. I must be the author, I thought. To be certain, taking my time, I wrote out the first sentence without looking back after I memorized it, so I would not subconsciously imitate the writing. I wrote, *It is possible to regard the following events in more than one way.* Again, when I compared the sentence to the beginning of the story, I was convinced that I had written the same words previously. I decided to write out the entire work. I thought that a sequential reconstruction of the text might stimulate my memory. This whole set of circumstances was very puzzling and troubling to me. After all, I must have been someone. I must have done things and went places and, for all I knew, I could have grown up in this very town. No one who had spoken to me so far recognized me or knew who I was. I did not know this Ambrogino; why would I have written about him? I flipped the pages until I reached the end of the story, and found that the journal still had many unused pages. I decided to begin again, and rewrote the first sentence as before....

It is possible to regard the following events in more than one way. To deny that possibility would be the same as erroneously accepting that something, whatever it may be, is always truly and completely itself because that is the form in which we experience it. I do not wish to convert the nonbeliever into a disciple. A voice can give comfort only to those who listen. An image can be understood only by those who see it. Telling the story of Ambrogino is something that I am compelled to do. I do not understand the reason. The war brought misery to countless souls. Just as in centuries past, the war took the lives of men, women, and children, by the thousands if not the millions, just as it will in centuries to come. The selection of Ambrogino, in the aftermath of this war, and in this time and place, is as incidental as it is predetermined. It is the median value between these opposites that I wish to identify. That is the substance that lies at the heart of the story of Ambrogino.

blows where it likes, and you hear
but cannot tell where it comes from
is every one that is born of the Sp

Someone, probably one of the priests or vergers, had written these ancient words on a broken, rectangular blackboard that was hung lengthwise to the right of the church entrance. Bombs had blown away part of the roof and removed the sides of the blackboard, while the block of incomplete scripture remained. Inside, an altar boy was lighting candles. There was chalk dust on his hands. He may have transcribed Christ's dictum, following the instructions of a superior, for the benefit of the faithful. The handwriting was elegant. There was a supply truck that had backed up to the church. The vehicle had a circular mirror that, in inverted form, partially reproduced the holy message. In its entirety the text read:

"The wind blows where it likes, and you hear the sound of it, but cannot tell where it comes from and where it goes. So is every one that is born of the Spirit." Ambrogino and his dog were passing through the courtyard. Some laughing children were playing nearby.

Their laughter was sarcastic and shrill. Surrounded by the high stone walls of multiple dwellings, the sounds the children produced reverberated with a slight echo. Behind the windows were people of various ages. Incomplete families, missing a deceased or absent father or son; a raped mother or daughter; a disoriented uncle or grandmother, driven mad by the war. Functional behavior, such as ironing a garment or watering a plant, occurred alongside irrational behavior. In one of the apartments was the grandfather of two brothers killed in the war. He sat on the edge of his bed while his wife washed him with a warm, damp cloth. He spent most of his time counting his footprints made in the dust of the rooms as he walked back and forth at random and mumbled unintelligible curses at God. In the floor below was a young woman who had been recently informed of her husband's death. She accepted this fact with a strange insouciance that she could not understand and to compensate for what she feared was callousness she refused to remove the man's boots from their place beside the front door, as though they would be needed before he left on some neighborhood errand. It is not uncommon for the living to cling to physical reminders of the dead. The young wife was disturbed by ordinary sounds and the memory of her husband's voice. The dog's footprints were small but they were visible in the dirt. The animal's owner left footprints, too. One child threw a stone. From one of the open windows in the wall someone yelled "Stop that!" or "Show respect!"

I paused here to consider why I chose both phrases to express the displeasure of the person in the window who was yelling at the children. Could it be that, if I was in fact a witness to these events, and I had written this account sometime afterwards, my memory had failed me, and I simply could not be sure which phrase had been used? It could very well be that several persons observed this mistreatment of the unfortunate Ambrogino and so two different things may have been said, more or less simultaneously, by two different people. So far, in reading the story, I still had no recollection of this Ambrogino, or his dog, yet there was something familiar about him; as if he was a mist that, very slowly, was beginning to assume more corporeal dimensions. Yet the time and place and circumstances of his existence remained a mystery to me. I continued writing…

It was a poor district. A large pot filled with boiling water stood on the stove in one of the shabby apartments. There was no meat or fish or fowl. The meal that had to be cooked would consist of a few vegetables. Their color was unhealthy. On the kitchen table was a knife with a broken handle. In the corner was a pile of glass shards that had been swept into a heap that resembled a little cone of quartz, the remains of a kitchen window that had shattered during artillery fire. The sun shone through the empty frame upon the glass and made it appear to be incandescent, as though embers burned at the bottom of the shape. A man with an extremely swollen, bandaged foot was lying on a bed across from the window. Flour dust covered some of the black tiles in front of the stove. Chewing rodents had left little openings at the bottom of the large burlap sack that contained the fine white powder. All of this could be seen through what may have been the window from which the man or the woman had just shouted. Or the reprimand to the child who threw the stone at Ambrogino may have come from another window leading into another apartment.

More uncertainty. More ambiguity. Still puzzled by the possibility of more than one version of events, I strove to determine what motivated my decision to write these lines. Could it be that my impressions of this tenement were so subjective, that in my mind there was a swirl or a matrix of information, so that emotion and imagination governed the selection of detail, rather than the limited realities of physical perspective and the logic of identity? Did my sense of Ambrogino affect the depiction of reality, even the nature of reality; was Ambrogino a kind of *zeitgeist*, rather than a person, that characterized everything around him? I began to remember little pieces of activity in my life. Nothing conclusive, but more and more flashes of scenes, of things that must have happened before. I knew that I had studied modern painting. Suddenly I had an image of *Mystery and Melancholy of a Street* by de Chirico. Were the repeating archways and windows, descending in perspective, and the silhouette of the little girl with her hoop, visual triggers in my mind? Did these triggers allow the uncertainty of which apartment window, which reprimanding adult, to remain unresolved on the page I had written? Did the very act of writing become a way for me to question what was or was not possible?

Ambrogino and his dog were often ridiculed, mostly by children and sometimes by adults. Everyone was poor but Ambrogino was especially poor and the wretchedness of his existence triggered this mistreatment by those who, destitute themselves, felt compelled to belittle someone even less fortunate. It was a cruel impulse, motivated by self-preservation, which somehow justified itself because humanity under great duress will always revert to the atavism of the predator and the prey.

Ambrogino's footprints were unevenly spaced because of his lame gait. The child's stone nicked the bone of the dog's hind leg. It yelped at the same instant that the sickly carrots and potatoes were dropped into the pot with a splash that turned into a hiss as some of the water overflowed onto the hot stove. In the next room a crying child refused to be consoled.

Many of the bombed out buildings were barely habitable and since the end of the war there were those who had managed with improvised dwellings. Ambrogino fell into this category. In one of the last standing structures at the edge of the town he had secured a couple of rooms. Here nothing was available other than shelter. Once a week he walked into town for fresh water. Often during these trips the children's aim would land a stone or two into his bucket. On those occasions the water would burst out suddenly, either staining Ambrogino's trousers or wetting the dog's fur. This did not happen today. For cooking he made small fires behind the building. For light he searched the streets for broken, discarded candles. For warmth he wrapped himself (and his dog when the animal allowed it) with newspaper. And for now, at least, there was no immediate worry about warmth because it was the beginning of spring. The people were weary, emaciated and sick, but the renewed trees bloomed with green. Birds even landed on Ambrogino's windowsill from time to time. He left them breadcrumbs when he could. The moonlight trickling into the room collected in a corner and deposited a faint glow upon one of Ambrogino's boots. The birds flew away suddenly when the dog barked. Its nails grazing the wooden floor gave a metallic quality to its footfalls. At night Ambrogino's convulsive, incessant coughing kept the animal awake. Rarely would it abandon its post at the foot of his bed and go to sleep elsewhere.

It was indeed pitiful that in his old age Ambrogino should find himself alone except for his dog, foraging through ruins for food. At least some of the townspeople had more substantial resources. Some of the families had young men returning from duty with their service pay. Some of them owned small businesses that they were painstakingly reviving. For those with some money stored away, there was the black market. Ambrogino was viewed by many as something of a parasite. Or it could have been that his disheveled appearance, his utter poverty, the filthy dog that accompanied him everywhere and his abnormal walk made him a natural object of derision, a living reminder of the ravages they had suffered and wished desperately to forget. In any event, kindness towards Ambrogino was infrequent. The supply of stones was inexhaustible since there was wreckage and devastation everywhere. On windy nights particles of debris swept through the chimney in Ambrogino's room. These tiny fragments produced a faint, rattling sound. Masses were beginning to be held again but since the church roof had been blown apart, the prayer books absorbed the stubborn glow of unfiltered moonlight. Left unsupervised, some of the younger children teased each other with parts of a split wooden cross.

Ambrogino had lived in this town his entire life. From the time he had been a small boy, long before the war, until his old age now, just after the war. His parents had died long ago. They had owned a pharmacy and when Ambrogino was twelve, he began to help his father there. He was fascinated by all the bottles filled with different colored liquids. He loved the little bell or Chinese wind chimes that announced each customer's entrance into the shop.

Was I assuming Ambrogino's point of view as an old man? It would surely follow that, given his advanced age at the beginning of this story, if the object and the kind of noise produced by the object were being remembered by Ambrogino, there could be some uncertainty about the identity of this object, and the character of the sounds it produced. I remembered something about my childhood. I must have had a bicycle. I remembered the little bell that was fastened to the right handlebar. I had an image of my thumb pressing the side of the bell; pushing a little flat lever that made the bell ring. But I had written *or Chinese wind chimes* as well. As my mind began to reach back into itself, I continued to experience many elliptical sequences of blurry information, such as this image of myself as a child riding a bicycle. I knew, for example, that I rode the bicycle to school; I saw my father going to work at the university; he was a professor of literature; my mother loved gardening; she was also very fond of mobiles and wind chimes; we had one such chime, made of colored, tiny rectangles of glass, hanging in the kitchen, near the back door. As I read and wrote out the sentences, a greater and deeper sense of synchronicity took hold of me; there was a relationship between things and memories and people and places, inside and outside of this text, but so far the meaning that united these elements eluded my conscious understanding.

Late at night, when he could not sleep, which seemed to happen more and more often these days, probably because of the terrible coughing fits, he listened to the wind rustling the new leaves in the trees and thought he could hear the sound of the bell. But he knew this was the influence of memory and imagination. It was not perceptual. And yet, often enough, he would look over at his dog when the thin, distant music of the chime or the bell sounded through the empty night, as if the animal's lack of reaction proved that the sound was illusory. Ambrogino might have been waiting for a reaction, to prove that the sound was real. But the animal slept soundly enough, and the only thing Ambrogino noticed was the steady, rhythmic undulation of its breast, and occasionally its paw twitching in sleep. He wondered if dogs dreamt of things, too. Surely, thought Ambrogino, it was possible, that the dog, having seen so much violence and heard so much frightening noise, might be capable of dreaming about its death, if it were possible for the dog to regard itself in such a self-reflexive way. Ambrogino wondered about his own death. Each night he wondered if he would die in his sleep, if he could sleep. He wondered what would become of his dog, should he die. Huge bomb craters behind the building glinted under the sunlight that illuminated the metal debris scattered about. The dog's bark resounded when Ambrogino let it play there. The amplification of the bark was like the children's laughter but without their malice. It would be a good place to die, he thought. He did not want to die in his house. His father had died in their house. The men had come from the hospital and carried his father away on a stretcher. A large white sheet covered the body. This frightened Ambrogino more than the thought that his father was dead. It seemed to Ambrogino that the sheet made his father a stranger, someone who did not belong in his own house anymore, someone who no longer possessed an identity, someone who had to be taken away. Ambrogino did not want the dog to see him that way. More than likely, it was a silly thought. What possible difference could it make to the dog?

In spite of his infirmity, Ambrogino was lately in the habit of climbing the several flights of steps to the roof of his building so he could look at the night sky. Naturally the stairwell was pitch-black and Ambrogino struggled with a dripping candle in one hand and a cane in the other hand. With a light but certain step held in check by Ambrogino's shuffling form, the dog ascended behind him. The cane was fashioned from a wooden post and a large piece of cork at the tip served as a handle. Occasionally a drop of liquefied wax fell upon the stone and almost instantaneously flattened and hardened. When the timing was right the long sharp nails of the dog scraped the wax off the step before it could solidify. Although there were few steps, Ambrogino paused two or three times before making it to the roof. At these moments there was only the clogged sound of his difficult breathing and the aimless patter of the sniffing dog pacing back and forth on the charred landing. As he raised the candle to get a better view of the next step, the shadows of man and dog swept along the wall, widened and distorted by the angle of his hand and the movement of the flame.

Ambrogino greatly enjoyed the night sky. He was comforted by the gleam of the heavenly bodies. There were very few clouds and the clarity of all the constellations was striking. Ambrogino sat in his favorite spot, a broken wheelbarrow that for some inexplicable reason had been left on the roof. He had used the winter's supply of newspaper for a cushioned seat and a scorched wooden door for a back support. Circular areas of charred wood alternated with lighter, unburned patches, forming shapes that suggested some kind of large, budding flower. A shaft of moonlight shone through the empty circle that used to contain the knob. The tube of white light, occasionally broken in its fixed position when the dog darted across its path, shot across the roof like a flashlight beam when Ambrogino lifted himself from the chair. He would experience a moment of confusion when he sat down again and the halo disappeared, until he realized his own body was blocking the source of light.

Ambrogino felt a wonderful peacefulness here, under the serene moonlight, sitting beneath the stars. After some initial explorations, the dog would settle down, nestling against the cool metal of the wheelbarrow, not far from Ambrogino's feet. Sometimes a scurrying water bug would be revealed if it crossed a path of moonlight, and the dog would become alert, jerking its head and staring at the insect with fixed attention. Sometimes the animal would not stir at all, sighing lazily as Ambrogino patted its head.

As the weather became warmer, groups of children, especially the older children, began loitering among the ruins, even here, at the outskirts of the town. Their shouts preceded them, and bottles could be heard shattering against the burnt structures, or windows could be heard cracking apart from the stones. When he heard these disturbances he stiffened in his improvised easy chair, and the dog growled just audibly enough to give Ambrogino further cause for alarm. On such occasions Ambrogino had to determine whether or not the wind swirling through the leafy trees or the infrequent remote bursts of artillery fire had deceived him and created the illusion of the children's approach.

And so on this evening when the faint impact of glass splintering against some surface registered itself in first the dog's, and then Ambrogino's consciousness, the old man knew that the marauding pack was on its way. Ambrogino grasped the cork handle of his cane and struggled to lift himself from the wheel-barrow. At the same moment, one of the children, a boy of about fourteen with dirty hands and a long snake-like scar covering his right arm, spat vigorously at a sick cat. It had jumped out of the wreckage and darted for shelter into a scorched pocket-book sandwiched between some bricks. Already the dog stood barking into the cool black space of the rooftop doorway, spinning around to look at Ambrogino, then turning to the stairway, possibly as a way of encouraging Ambrogino to hurry towards the exit, possibly as a way of instinctively protecting him from imminent danger. The exact intention of the animal was not clear, but Ambrogino struggled nevertheless, limping across the roof, grasping his make-shift cane with the same fierceness as an older boy who just then stepped over and drove a long, carefully sharpened stick into the pocket book, piercing the cat's throat and pinning it firmly to the ground. The mangy front claws of the animal jutted through the handbag. Outstretched stiffly, they twitched slightly during death throes. The blood streaked down from the wound, staining the matted fur. The movement of the blood, however slow, contrasted with the stillness of the death stare.

There were cries of "Hooray for the Victor!" or "Down with the Invader!" as the boys stomped around the cat's corpse, their strong, youthful voices echoing throughout the hollow landscape. The wind shook the trees. It seemed as though the boys' voices blended with the breeze.

I may have wandered through this town for weeks or even months. Such phrases were rather dramatic and a little simplistic; one could imagine a group of children shouting something like *Down with the invader!* or *Hooray for the Victor!* as a way of celebrating some perceived accomplishment in warfare that they did not fully understand.

One could imagine the even greater likelihood that, in their characteristic and unfortunate imitation of the words and deeds of adults, the children were simply re-enacting, with a bravura that was pitiful in its glorification of killing, the execution of a prisoner of war or a soldier felled by a sniper's bullet. I suppose I could have remembered such phrases because of my contact with the town, moving in and around areas where the voices of children could be heard. I was not sure.

The boys' circling movements appeared upon a dusty panc of glass in a shaky window frame. The wind snapped against the loose wood. The amorphous image of the chanting boys collapsed like a puzzle tableau falling from a table as the window glass shattered into fragments. Startled by the loud, splintering sound, some large, dark birds leapt in unison from the ledge of the building. Their black wings flapped under the chalky moon. The old man puffed with exhaustion as he descended the stairs. His minuscule torch flickered slightly. In contrast, the boy's eyes, the one who had harpooned the cat, glowed with energy. The prompt of the dog's nervous bark preceded Ambrogino at every landing as he slowly made his way down the stairs. Awkwardly lowering the candle to his hip, his face was eventually overtaken by shadow.

The boy with the peculiar scar licked a sore on his upper lip. Another child struggled with a stone too heavy to lift. He may have wanted to use it to crush the skull of the cat.

Because of the viciousness of their actions, the ugly thrill they experienced from destroying life, I suppose it would be reasonable to assume that any object in the boys' hands, such as the heavy stone, could be used as a weapon, something to cause more destruction and death. As I wrote these sentences, I remembered a scene from my childhood. Some of the older boys had taken me to a vacant lot, where an old, stray dog was often to be found. They beat it to death with discarded, rusty pipes. They ran away, laughing at me, because I could only stand there, holding my length of filthy pipe, sobbing. I could not participate in such a sickening act. Later that night, when the other boys were long gone, I returned to the lot with a shovel I had taken from my father's garage. I dug a hole and buried the poor creature. This memory could be the reason that I have become fond of Ambrogino's dog. I felt a great anxiety over my powerlessness to help it.

The fleeing birds glided over these boys who were so perversely energized by having hunted and killed. The knife used to cut the unappealing vegetables now lay on the washboard in the semi-darkened kitchen. There were droplets of water on the dull blade. The cranky child who had cried for so long slept soundly. He clutched the rag doll that had served as a calmative. There was dried saliva on the doll's awkwardly stitched, faded cloth face. Ambrogino, drenched in sweat, shut his door behind him and rested his chin on the spongy cork of his cane, tasting his salty perspiration, listening for breaking glass and angry voices. The dog anxiously paced in circles within the debris filled room, occasionally stopping to bark at the window which overlooked the bomb crater behind the building.

The boys were filled with blind rage and cruelty. No one in their path tonight would be safe, unless it was a strong, armed adult who could threaten them equally, and intimidate them into obedience consistent with their long lost adolescence. Ambrogino was especially vulnerable to such attacks. Certainly it was disgraceful that his old age and his afflictions made him a target for such violence. They lifted their heads and turned toward Ambrogino's building. They spoke again and said what they were going to do but their words were not intelligible. They were making unalterable decisions.

I wondered, as I did over previous parts of the text, why I would create an ambiguity here, to make the content of the boys' comments unknown, referring instead to their words as unintelligible. Having written this much of the story over, thoroughly convinced that I was the author, it occurred to me, at first, that, like the earlier examples, this could be considered a dichotomy of style. Apparently, I had chosen an authorial or omnipotent point of view; therefore, how could the words spoken by the boys not be known to the narrator? Was I thinking, subconsciously, of that day when the unfortunate dog was slaughtered? The other boys ran off, exchanging laughs and insults at my expense, but their voices became more distant as they ran, and as they vanished from earshot, I could not distinctly hear their words.

A group of soldiers were slowly patrolling the area. Their purpose was to maintain security at night; prevent looting, disturbances, assaults. Much of the crime committed recently had been attributed to these boys and this unit had been dispatched principally to intercept them. There was mud on the men's boots and their field helmets were dusty. One of them held the remains of a long extinguished cigarette between his lips while listening to his sergeant colorfully describe a sexual adventure he had had the previous evening. Part of a cracked brick fell among the debris as the frightened birds flew to another rooftop. Instantly the men swung out their weapons, pointing in the direction of the sound. The final days of the war had made the soldiers' survival instincts so acute that even the remotest possibility of danger produced an alarmed response. It may have been that, having lived through all that they had experienced, they were particularly leery that some unforeseen minor incident could rob them of their lives now that the war was officially over. Once they recognized the source of the noise, they relaxed themselves with professional control: no unnecessary shots fired. The soldier finally ignited his cigarette as the promiscuous Sergeant resumed, in mid-sentence, the account of his conquest the prior evening. It was with a shopkeeper's tubercular daughter who cooked him a modest meal afterwards. He did not use her fork when she offered it. The soldier was a medic and quite familiar with the smell of blood. It may have been his awareness of the woman's affliction that caused him to imagine that he smelled the remains of dried blood everywhere in the house. She listened to the heavy footfalls of his combat boots on the cobblestones as she lit a cigarette in the dim kitchen. She did not consider herself a prostitute though she had sex with some of the soldiers in order to get money for food. She knew this man. They had grown up together and he did not remember her. She refused his money and was far too ashamed to summon some common experiences from their childhood that might trigger a recollection.

The young wife had postponed the task of going through her dead husband's clothes and tonight she decided to be done with it. His military uniforms had been returned to her and there were also many articles of civilian clothing hanging in the closet. She brought everything over to the kitchen table so she could work more conveniently. A brass button from one of his dress jackets smacked hard against the wooden table and she was startled by the sound. The contents of his pockets were predictable: cigarettes, a few coins, some enemy trophies such as bullets or small knives, letters that he had received from her, and one letter to her that had not been sent. This couple had no children and because so many neighbors had scattered as the war reached its conclusion, the woman had no occasion to speak to anyone in the prior few weeks. She had been storing food and water for some time, and there had been no need to go about looking for supplies. She opened the letter and read it aloud and was surprised at the sound of her own voice, realizing that this was the first time she had spoken in the apartment without speaking to her husband.

The grandfather went into a sudden rage and demanded to know who had stolen his footprints. He stood on top of his dilapidated bed, balancing his shaking body by bracing one arm against the wall as he shook his other fist at invisible thieves who always seemed to come in the night and remove most of his footprints. His wife was accustomed to these episodes. She sat on the bed and reassured the shouting man that he had merely miscounted, and all of his footprints were still there. After a brief period during which the old man suspected that his wife was an impostor, he began to calm himself somewhat, and eventually, reaching for him as delicately as possible, the wife persuaded him to lower himself back into his bed. "It's the enemy! They did this! Don't you understand, they're taking away my footprints and we've got to get them back!" warned the man as his wife guided him back under the bedding and tried to make him comfortable though his head rarely touched the pillows as he spoke with urgency. In the morning, she cajoled, they would look together in the daylight and find every footprint. The man was very concerned; he explained again and again that he was tracing a pathway to heaven for his grandsons, and he wanted to make sure they could find it, otherwise who knew what would become of their souls. His wife stroked his hair. She discreetly shook her head, as if silently discussing her husband's sorrowful state with herself, the way decent passers-by feel a fleeting shame at their wholeness when confronted by the handicapped. He suspected the enemy of stealing his footprints and using them to deceive the two young men. This had to be prevented at all costs, he stated. He had fought in the previous war, and he knew how insidious the enemy could be. All of that would be fixed in the morning, cooed his exhausted wife, when the sun was up again and, if she could find wood for the stove, the smell of her coffee filled the rooms. And as always, she reassured, they would look for the footprints together.

The altar boy sat on the front pew eating an orange. Some fresh fruit had become available recently through the black market. He remembered his mother's habit of taking the orange peels and placing them over the pilot light at the center of the stove, to create the sweet, wafting aroma of orange throughout the apartment. The peels lay beside him, carefully piled one upon another. He lived with his aunt, and he thought, maybe now that the war was over, it may no longer be so dangerous to visit his mother's grave. They had buried her in another town, in the same part of the cemetery that contained the graves of her parents. He often thought of the last words he heard his mother say, on the day she took the train to visit her ailing brother. Later that day there had been an air-raid and the railroads were bombed. She was always teasing her son about his parrot. She knew how much he liked to talk to the bird, and the pleasure he took when, after much repetition, the creature finally mastered the high-pitched reproduction of a word or a little phrase. She was most proud of her son's interest in the church and encouraged him to consider the priesthood. Yet she was playful about it when in connection to the parrot. They kissed good-bye on the train platform and she told her son what to say to the bird. She wanted to be surprised when she came back and heard the parrot repeat the phrase.

"You must teach it to say, 'God knows the future with as much certainty as He knows the present.'"

"But Mama, that is too long! He cannot remember it all! What can I do?"

She laughed and hugged him. She expected no less than complete success, for she believed in him. He remembered the scent of her perfume against his cheek and for some reason he associated that smell with the orange in his hands. The two smells were not at all alike. In the rectory hung the boy's street clothes and stuffed into the back pocket of his pants was the perch bar from the parrot's cage.

Down the road from the church was a hospital that overflowed with wounded soldiers as well as civilians of all ages. In the basement, where the laundry was done, were hundreds of green military blankets covered with dark red stains. There were many patches of dried blood on the wooden floors of the operating rooms, where the emergency surgery had been performed. A source of much post-operative infection could be traced to this wooden floor. Imbedded between the planks was a potentially lethal, soft material, which had accumulated over the months from dropped surgical instruments and soaked cotton pads. This had become a rich breeding ground for Streptococci bacteria and many patients suffered from serious post-operative infections. A young doctor, pondering the idea of pulling up the boards and laying down a cement floor, sat at his desk and stared at his hands.

Many older horses had succumbed to strangles disease. There were few opportunities for proper isolation and contagion was rampant. Horse owners reached the point where, to protect the remainder of their herds, even the bridal equipment was discarded and burned. A large disposal procedure had been underway for some time and now, with some semblance of order having returned to the town, it continued without interruption. Dozens of horse carcasses had been hauled by cart and truck to an enormous mass grave dug in the woods. Each day, another equine corpse was deposited there. To consolidate space, the bodies were laid to rest in an upside down position, so that the stiffened legs of the animals jutted upwards. In this way the beasts could be laid out side by side. Many villagers, after depositing their load, came away from the sight with the impression of a sunken forest, thinking of the long, once powerful brown and black legs as narrow trees reaching toward the sky.

The wind suddenly swept through the trees; it produced a sucking sound, like an unclogged drain. The rustling and shaking of leaves shaped a rhythm not unlike the succession of knocking sounds as Ambrogino was pulled down the last flight of steps. The laughing boys gripped his legs and there was blood everywhere. An arabesque of smaller and smaller red circles appeared from landing to landing. The blood was smeared by Ambrogino's collar and the dotted steps of the excitedly barking dog, its snapping bites soon to be stilled by the boy with the scar. The stick's sharpened point was thrust with precision and great velocity but the dog slipped unexpectedly on its master's blood. The animal escaped the spear, which imbedded itself in the wooden balustrade. The end of the slender projectile vibrated after impact. The staccato report of military rifles transformed into dozens of scattering footsteps as the boys fled in separate directions.

Ambrogino had succumbed to unconsciousness as a result of the mortal wounds to his head. He lay on his back and his breathing became lighter and fainter with each moment. This supine position, given the gravity of his head wounds, must have accelerated the bleeding. Swirls of blood leaked from both sides of his skull, circling around and curving into a kind of floral pattern. Expanding into double shapes that mimicked the effect of time-elapse photography, when an imperceptibly blooming flower is shown in fast motion, the bunched areas of blood rapidly opened and spread forward.

Ambrogino was buried in the bomb crater behind his house. There was no sense of decency or ceremony in his burial: the body was wrapped and covered with lime to hasten decomposition. Disease and infection were still a public health concern and the unburied dead were disposed of quickly. The dog could not be found. There were no footprints. There were no reflections. There were no shadows. There was no one to mourn for Ambrogino. No one wept for him. There could be an epiphany, an image in which a child, an old woman, and a young man stood at his grave.

I remembered the death of my grandfather. I must have been around seven years old. I was so fond of him; he told me stories, took me along when he met his cronies for a drink, always knew how to make me laugh. When he died, my father asked me, during the wake at the funeral parlor, if I wanted to remember him as he was, or did I want to go into the room, with the intense smell of so many flowers, and the muffled sobs that I kept hearing, and see him in his coffin. We stood, my father and I, just a few feet from the entrance to the chapel that contained my grandfather's body, in his coffin, and there was an elderly woman, probably a relative or friend, standing alongside us, preparing to pay her respects inside. I told my father that I wanted to keep my memory of my grand-father as it was; I knew there would be something incomprehensibly illusory about seeing him that way, looking at his dead body, as if he was pretending to be someone else, or something else, and the illusion would not go away, and he could not wake up and say things or do things anymore. In my mind, remembering his stories, picturing him laughing and walking, there were no restrictions against what my grandfather could do, and I liked seeing him that way. Memory is a strange tool of the mind; it watches over you with its endless supply of images and sounds, yet it can torment you with reminders of loss, or, as in my case, leave you somewhere dark and imaginary, and refuse to answer when called.

Somehow in dealing with their own hardship and misfortune during the war, they had come to know Ambrogino. In spite of their personal tragedy and sorrow (the child, for example, had lost her mother during a bombing), they felt compassion for Ambrogino and showed him kindness. When one of the children who belonged to the group of children who so often laughed cruelly at Ambrogino and flung stones at him, had absconded with his water bucket, the young man, having witnessed this, ran after the insensitive child, retrieving the pail and giving it back to Ambrogino. The old woman remembered Ambrogino's politeness and smile. When she was a little girl, she had visited the pharmacy with her parents and Ambrogino had secretly given her a sweet when his father was not looking. Although it had been more than sixty years earlier, she could still see the little square of fudge that the boy had surreptitiously stuffed into the blue pocket of her white dress. The candy was wrapped in shiny gold paper and had some kind of white scroll-like design. She thought of her own mortality and of all the dead; finally she thought of the little boy who had been kind to her long ago. She found herself amazed that the corpse in the hole before her was in any way connected to the image of the boy inside her head. That image flashed back and forth; it dipped behind little moments and shadows; lifted itself over time and shimmered with the immediacy of fresh paint or a new coin. She turned away and slowly made her way back to the courtyard where Ambrogino often walked with his water pail and his dog. She passed the church and made the sign of the cross as she looked in puzzlement at the blackboard.

blows where it likes, and you hear
but cannot tell where it comes from
is every one that is born of the Sp

I remembered. I understood. The inconsistencies in the text were a kind of literary manifestation of the wind, described in the parable.

You hear the sound of it, but cannot tell where it comes from and where it goes. That in the analogy of wind and Spirit, many mysteries of life are conjured, many possible connections between man and God are suggested. That like the wind, the Spirit is sovereign; the Spirit is invisible. Like the wind, the Spirit is inscrutable; incomprehensible; indispensable; life-giving…irresistible. I was deeply interested in the metaphysics of language. I had studied art and literature before I trained at the seminary for the priesthood. I was an army Chaplain. I wrote quite often. I rarely slept and tried to keep myself occupied by writing stories. I visited Ambrogino once, after one of the stone-throwing attacks committed by the children, to offer him some consolation and to see if he required medical attention. The sorrows of his life had touched me. Then, a few months later, I had learned of his death. Although it was not my calling or responsibility, I decided to write the story of Ambrogino, at least in as much as I could imagine what the scope of his life might have been. I suppose it was not difficult to insert the missing pieces, given what I did know of his day to day existence. And yet, in becoming the creator of a self-enclosed world that contained Ambrogino in the purest sense, I felt empowered by invention and language and, most of all, the possibility of free will. I wanted the text to become two seemingly contradictory things: the voice of an other-worldly creator who allowed His beings to make choices yet already knew what those choices would be, and a man-made tale that somehow achieved an incantatory power, like the apocryphal story of the rich old man who offered five guineas to a sailor to impregnate his wife. I believed that language could elevate Ambrogino beyond what he was in life; as though he might acquire a symbolic significance, like the warnings of Ignorance and Want embodied by the pitiful children under the robe of the second apparition. To offer him up as a kind of metaphorical sacrifice; as a condemnation of the senselessness and horror of war, as an embodiment of the suffering it caused. I was discharged shortly after I wrote the story; I left the church soon afterwards and did volunteer work at a hospital in another town. I was there for the past two years. I lost my memory in that town. There was an explosion from artillery fire. I was standing near a window, lost my balance, and fell out. Luckily, I was on the first floor. I must have wandered over here at some point and lost consciousness in one of the buildings. Troops, especially medical and religious officers, were always changing and moving around, so nobody here recognized me. Certainly, Ambrogino's murder was a horrific event. Nothing could be done about that. Yet there was elegance and beauty in this image of it. It was a poetic image. I knew that he died violently; that the vicious tribe of ravaging boys was responsible. I thought that comparing the flow of his blood to some kind of floral shape or pattern, given the hideousness of his death (I was told that his features were unrecognizable), would create a lyrical dimension, a moment of epiphany for Ambrogino. Certainly there was very little, if anything, in any part of Ambrogino's life, especially this final part of his life, which could be even remotely called poetic. At least Ambrogino's death, as a beautiful image, might somehow be gracefully and mercifully juxtaposed against the meanness and starkness of his life. That was my intention. My hope now is that the results are in harmony with my aspirations. In granting freedom to that which is created, while the creation seems at times to have a life of its own, certain secrets are somehow concealed from the created. At the same time, the knowingness of the Creator may be mysteriously compromised, because moments of the image, and the life they hold, may transform or move in unexpected directions. There was a window next to my bed. I was on the third floor of the hospital. I picked up the pen and wrote....

From a window in his room the altar boy saw a dog in the street. Its fur appeared to be stained with blood.

Dear Father Cosmo,

I shall be pleased to discuss with you some specific subjects for the paintings that have been commissioned. I expect to arrive in California next month. I'm sure that you are fully joyful that the Holy Father has granted permission for some religious paintings, perhaps including a fresco, for your beloved parish. I shall meet you for lunch as we previously arranged.

Yours In Christ,

Domenico Tojetti

Patience is the Companion of Wisdom

Father Cosmo, like many people in their early forties, had discovered one day that he could no longer read without the aid of eyeglasses. The priest preferred a large magnifying glass. He used it whenever he went through correspondence at his desk in the rectory alongside the church. A letter of great importance had arrived recently and he had left the heavy thick instrument on top of it while he prepared for morning mass. The shapes of the inked words became enlarged and distorted, like the dissected particles of an insect viewed on a slide under a microscope, because the convex surface of the glass rested so close to the handwritten page.

A teenaged boy, overcome with anger and sorrow, had recently ventilated his rage towards the church by firing his .22 Smith & Wesson at its stained chapel windows. The boy appeared one evening with his rifle and began shooting; he had learned that day that both of his older brothers had died in Texas at the battle of Sabine Pass. Fortunately, because of the small caliber of the bullets, the panes did not shatter. There were, however, scattered holes circumscribed by web-thin cracks in the rainbow rich colors of the panels. Sunlight streamed through these little circles and overlapping chinks in the chapel glass. Suspended geometric shapes, a sprinkling of cylinders and trapezoids projected onto the dark confessional wood, made the smooth mahogany surface resemble a jumbled puzzle, filled with white pieces that would not fit.

Sitting on a bench inside the murky booth, Father Cosmo adjusted his position, causing his severely starched, black clerical clothing to make rustling sounds that were amplified by the enclosed space and evoked a bundle of papers cascading from a shelf. The thirty-three buttons of the cassock, representing the earthly life of Christ, were particularly vexing to Father Cosmo this morning; his fingers kept slipping on them in the soggy sea mist that permeated every surface in his rectory quarters. He was annoyed and dressed with impatience. Being especially sensitive to heat, the priest greatly missed his previous parish on the east coast. The tuft of his biretta had wilted from the steamy air; the square, black hat rested on a little stool next to the priest's handsome, oak armoire, a gift donated by the town's funeral director.

When Father Cosmo visited parishioners in the town, his mind became preoccupied with the noise of the busy streets. There was something about the relationship between movement, sound, and silence that had an inordinately powerful effect on Father Cosmo's thoughts. Shop-owners waved at him from behind the glass windows of their stores and the large black lettering on the glass obscured his smiling face. Elderly townspeople, especially women, greeted him with great seriousness and dignity; they crossed themselves repeatedly and grasped his forearm with as much strength as their old hands could exert. At the confectioner's shop, where groups of children could be found regardless of the time of day, a circle of little boys and girls surrounded Father Cosmo and provoked gentle yet determined opposition from him as he struggled to keep their soiled hands away from his fresh clothing.

There was a small, gold woman's ring, with a rectangular, blue-green garnet, in Father Cosmo's cassock. It poked his flesh when he tried to cross his legs. He found it difficult to sit still. He kept forgetting that the edges of the ring-stone pressed against him at a painful angle; they pinched him again and again. The friction of the fabric irritated his skin. Some of the material had dampened from absorbing his perspiration. The humidity in the church made everything moist and sticky. The glaring, Indian summer sun was slowly burning the hazy, steamy air of the morning away. It was the middle of the week but already the pews were filled with many parishioners waiting to be absolved. From time to time a newcomer tried to squeeze into a space that was only a fraction of what was needed to accommodate someone adequately. The congregation sat in respectful, prayerful meditation, heads bowed, as if everyone had slumped into a state of sleep.

Signore Tojetti's lunch appointment with Father Cosmo was less than an hour away. They were to discuss the frescoes and other religious paintings that had been planned for the church. The Vatican held Domenico Tojetti in high esteem; he moved in powerful circles there and the fact that his transatlantic visit to America included an invitation to the priest of this small, isolated parish indicated good prospects for the curate's career. Before his trip, Signore Tojetti had finished an extensive restoration project at the Vatican. Father Cosmo appreciated the value of religious icons; he believed that images were important to Christianity and offered a method for understanding and preserving faith. Father Cosmo was scheduled to hear confessions all day; he wished instead that he was holding mass and giving communion. That way he wouldn't have to speak individually to each person, except to say *The body of Christ* as he placed the dry wafer on a slippery tongue. He sighed, quietly waiting for the penitent to finish his narrative. The meshed screen separating them vibrated slightly. On the other side was an old man who trembled with palsy and often used the little screen to brace his palm. Father Cosmo associated the shaking panel with a honeycomb faintly stirring with the movements of bees. He reminded himself that he was bound by duty to the old man, having heard his confessions for many years (particularly since the passing of the man's wife the previous winter), yet he could not refrain from making this comparison during their interviews. He tried to concentrate on the man's words, changing his posture once more to avoid the irritation of the jewelry in his pocket. He thought about the delicious seafood at the restaurant where he was to meet his guest. He knew that the European church, throughout medieval times, distributed the priests' leftover food to the poor. He imagined the lobsters being prepared at this very moment for the midday clientele and wondered if the church's charitable practice regarding food was still in effect.

"It's been so difficult these months. I think of her constantly. Everything she did for me...everything. I'm barely able to look after myself. I miss her company, her face, her voice. Why did she leave me?"

Another priest, looking through the chapel window, noticed how birds quickly filled the trees. Turning to the confessional, he saw the silhouette of a sparrow that suddenly appeared within one of the white patches of sunlight that emanated from the pockmarked glass. The bird's pecking gestures were jittery and animated and its semblance trembled upon the confessional cabinet, a delicate pantomime within one of the small, deformed configurations.

The old man's voice was weary with sorrow. The often-repeated statements, the often-asked questions were a challenge for Father Cosmo who always searched for something comforting to say during a confession. Yet in this case Father Cosmo recognized that there was nothing left to say. The old man and his wife had been together for almost fifty years. There were no children. He lived modestly but comfortably enough on his savings. Much to Father Cosmo's annoyance, the confessions had become a pretense for the man to state over and over his singular fear of being alone for the first time in his life. Since his wife's death the lonely widower, whose attendance at mass was far less than regular when the woman was alive, sometimes appeared twice in the same day, desperate to hear something comforting from Father Cosmo or, more likely, determined to enumerate his anxieties.

Father Cosmo, most confused by such behavior, thought that Christianity taught its followers to find courage in the promise of everlasting life. The old should understand this better than most, thought Father Cosmo. He would speak his thought, a bit harshly at times, whenever the old man, either because of his infirmity or stubbornness, did not reach for the confessional door to exit, even after Father Cosmo's repeated attempts to end the session.

Unfortunately, Father Cosmo suffered from a severe stammer; sometimes he could not find sufficient breath for clearly enunciated speech unless he spoke in a whisper. He found that he could overcome the embarrassing stutter only when his voice was no more than a murmur. At such times, especially when he was hearing confession, he spoke very quickly. This technique, which preserved the air required for clearly uttered speech, forced those who listened, such as the old man today, to lean closer and closer toward Father Cosmo, to capture the flow of words. As Father Cosmo spoke, the old man replaced his palm with his head, so his ear was pressed tightly against the screen and the divider ceased to quiver. In the silent, stuffy confessional, filled with crustacean-like outlines that reminded Father Cosmo of his growing hunger, the widower tried to absorb all that Father Cosmo said, and the old man hoped there was some element of insight or consolation that he had not heard on past occasions.

There was the faint jangle of metal falling against metal as a woman dropped her pennies into the poor box next to the tiered candle stand. As she crossed the aisle and returned to the pew, her back intercepted the sunbeams. Her hobbled gait made the incomplete triangles and rhomboids of light bobble slightly, until her shuffling body unblocked their path, allowing the rays to glance upon the wood.

Her stooped form was the result of having been a housekeeper most of her life. Luckily, she had found secure employment for many years in the home of a wealthy textile merchant. Her employer, a life-long bachelor, was a cold man who ate alone and was parsimonious both in his personal life and his accounts. While he had provided the woman with free room and board, her accommodations were slight. She lived in an attic apartment furnished with nothing more than a simple straw bed, a washstand, and a dilapidated bureau. The merchant was obsessed with cleanliness and order; his splendid home had wooden floors with elaborate parquetry that he wanted regularly waxed and polished. Hunched over the floors for hours at a time, the housekeeper gave the wood a beautiful sheen, moving up and down with the rhythm of her strokes as she applied the thick rag for her task.

Always a devout churchgoer, the housekeeper hoped that her recent prayers would be answered. The merchant had died and a nephew, who resembled him not only in appearance but personality, had summarily informed the woman that she must make new arrangements as soon as possible. The nephew, after learning about his uncle's death, had sold the house to the man's competitor. There had been some degree of animosity between this nephew and his aloof uncle, hence this arrangement that gave ownership of the merchant's home to a business rival. The new owner had, in fact, offered the housekeeper a position. Her prayer was that another offer might miraculously find her. This man, she learned, would rent the house; he wanted the housekeeper to travel with him, far away in the East, and provide her services at his urban townhouse. There was no element of compassion in this decision. The man despised his competitor so viciously that he wanted to somehow obliterate all traces of the dead man's existence. Renting the house and transferring the deceased's servant to unfamiliar surroundings was his way of making the man's life null and void, as though he had never been. Naturally the housekeeper, a spinster, hoped to finish her days with some familiar company, such as the small group of people she came to know in the town over time. She had become anxious and frightened and was almost sixty; suddenly nothing in her future was certain.

A bruised child averted the rigid brim of his father's black hat as he lit a candle for his recently deceased sister. The man dropped his rosary and it fell to the stone church floor, resounding like pebbles or shells. A cluster of tapers was imbedded in the scented ash. A man was lighting a series of candles to mark the anniversary of the death of a loved one. Returning to his seat, behind the first row of candles positioned at waist level, he watched the child step down from the candle stand, viewing him through the tapers, which acted as an obstruction in the manner of a picket fence. The boy wore short pants and the fresh bruises on his thighs were partially concealed by the thin, closely grouped sticks. Speaking through clenched teeth and digging with calloused fingers into the soft fabric of the hat, the boy's father commanded him to retrieve the rosary. The child noticed the white border of a photograph of the man's daughter that protruded from his jacket pocket. In an alcove set aside for the candles were several large statues of saints. Imposing figures with arms outstretched, their likeness appeared across the glossy paper because of the hundreds of candle flames in the gallery. These little torches, bending and twisting in all directions, gave the dark forms an eerie, restless mobility. The boy's father removed the photograph after the child sat down, as though the lighting of the candle for his daughter somehow authorized this public examination of the memento. In thc picture, which had been taken in front of a fireplace, there was a large kerosene lamp on the mantle behind the man's head. He stared at the camera with an expressionless gaze as he held his newborn daughter in his arms.

The man was a blacksmith and the harshness of his work seemed to have characterized his appearance and personality. He bent the fingers of his right hand as though his tool was always invisibly in his grasp. The man could not distinguish between the clang of steel that resonated even at night as he lay in bed and the rush of angry thoughts that would not leave his mind since the death from tuberculosis of his young daughter. He wanted to force the rage and despair out of himself the way he used the tools to impose a new shape upon the heated steel. Unfortunately, no one who knew him, least of all his easily frightened boy could understand that this roughness towards his son was his only protection against a numbing fear that this child, too, might fall sick and die. The man had been raised to believe that one must go to church to find consolation in God; that lighting a candle for the dead was important; that death was only a doorway to eternal life. He looked at no one and forgot to cross himself.

The silver tip of a cane for the blind snapped sharply against the aisle stone as a young man rose from the last pew. After whispering his litany of penance, he stepped confidently toward the center aisle, using his walking aid to guide himself from the church. Blind since birth, the young man, like many deprived of sight, had sharpened his remaining senses. Sound in particular had become a substitute for vision and he was astute in recognizing the identity and location of both things and people by listening to telltale characteristics of movement. He had memorized the number of steps between his house and the church. When he stepped from the boards onto the dirt, the sound of wagons guided his movements. Tapping the stick back and forth helped him walk in a straight line. The smell of pitch always let him know that he had almost reached his destination. There was a blacksmith's only one hundred yards from the church. The young man was especially fond of his sense of touch. The feel of soil was very pleasurable for him. There was a small vegetable garden at home and his mother helped him plant tomatoes and carrots. The young man kept his Braille copy of the New Testament in his room. The mud was cool and smelled pungent and the man often tried to imagine Jesus. He wondered what it would be like to see for the first time after Christ rubbed the mud on his eyes.

"And all the regrets I cannot escape...all the little things I cannot make up for anymore. The times I was cross with her, when I lied to her, or if I forgot to do a small kindness for her, when she had asked me for something."

Father Cosmo listened with a sense of duty, but the old man's words blended with the faint rumble of wagon wheels bouncing on the road just outside the church. The driver of the cart cracked his whip against the hindquarters of the tired horse as another priest busied himself at the altar, cleaning a chalice and other Eucharistic materials used during the previous mass. There were black double patches stitched upon the front of the priest's vestment, adorned with Latin inscriptions. Two black rectangles with rounded edges, the patches resembled the leather eye blinders that pacified the beast. With its vision artificially restricted, the animal pushed itself forward in response to the whip. The repeating mechanical swipe of its tail fanned away the buzzing flies hovering above its posterior as the priest wiped the wine stained cup with a linen cloth.

As the wagon was passing on the road, two elderly sisters, walking in unison, crossed themselves as they approached the stone steps of the church. Their ill-fitting high-laced boots were revealed when they arduously lifted complicated skirts over the long stones that radiated the oppressive late morning heat. At the same instant, the sun's brilliance infiltrated the foot of nude cherubim in the stained glass. Unencumbered by gravity, the figure floated in celestial space, gesturing towards earth with a merciful expression. The sisters had never married and lived together in a large house that belonged to their parents. Having grown up there, it was the only home they had known. One of the sisters was fond of painting; she did some needlepoint as well but arthritis and failing eyesight had caused her to abandon this pastime. Her painting continued. Scores of canvases, hung and stacked, could be found on the many walls and floors, throughout the rooms in the large house. Her favorite subjects, inspired again and again by visits to the church for mass as well as social events, were in fact the many depictions of cherubim and saints that were to be found in panel after panel of stained glass. The woman had a very unusual sense of detail, especially in creating a spatial context for her scenes. Most of the motifs in her canvasses showed the earth, blue and green and suspended in the universe, as a small ball. Next to the earth, dwarfing the planet would be one of the angels from the imposing and regal panels of stained glass. It did not occur to the artist to separate the angelic figure from its man-made, artfully constructed frame, or to paint it in realistic proportion to the earth, hence the gargantuan size of the figure. Thus the finished result was most peculiar in that it combined an awareness of the real position of earth in the solar system with the purely imaginary presence of a piece of religious imagery, shown in exaggerated scale.

The sisters, now very old, were well known in the town; though they had never joined the society outside of their home. Except for these trips to Sunday mass, they had no contact with anyone or any social function. They spoke only to each other and feared anything new. In return, the people who had seen them grow old or knew them only as old watched them pass by without sympathy. As little girls, more than seventy years ago, they had fed apples to the horses in their father's barn, played with wisps of straw, helped their mother bake pies. But their father's Calvinist obsession with moral purity left them no room for social mingling and emotional growth. Their ability to live and love died long before the dirt scattered over the lids of their parents' coffins. They had only the legacy of the painting, encouraged by their mother, a schoolteacher who tried to give her daughters a sense of beauty in the world.

Located less than a mile from the shore, the church was frequently buffeted by gales. Behind the rectory was a little garden littered with wood chips blown about from the prior night's storm. Some workers were doing repairs on the rectory and the blond shavings were scattered throughout the roses. As the wagon approached the church, a sharp sliver of wood flew in the garden, the result of a man using an axe to split some old beams. The tiny wooden spear nicked a grasshopper in mid-stride, immobilizing it underneath some rose bushes. The velvet green legs twisted helplessly in the sweet garden air. Some mockingbirds perched upon a large wooden cross in the rear of the garden.

Father Cosmo admitted to himself that his mind was indeed elsewhere today. He had been thinking for some time about his questionable conduct with a girl from a farm several miles away. After much formal meditation and painful introspection, he had decided that any form of profane love must not violate his life-long bond to the church. Such a violation must be avoided, whatever the cost. He reproached himself for allowing this hypocritical situation to perpetuate itself for so long, but he was relieved by the conversation he had had with the girl. During this recent meeting he informed her that he would end their meetings, that they would not see one another again. The girl was naive, poor, and ignorant: her infatuation with Father Cosmo was not surprising. She had fallen in love with his knowledge of ideas, of the world, his sophistication, his charms. Her inexperience and youth made her unprepared for his rejection, something which would have to be considered not only necessary but also inevitable. Only someone in Father Cosmo's position, who was fully aware of the unalterable bond between God and

His servants, could see such things clearly. Far more serious concerns were at stake, beyond the understanding of a lovesick child.

Patience is the companion of wisdom.

The quotation from Saint Augustine, something that Father Cosmo had often spoken to the young lady, was written on a little piece of green notepaper that the girl quietly handed to Father Cosmo before saying good-bye. She went through several rooms and closed each door so Father Cosmo could not hear her sob. On a bureau in the last room was the girl's display area for her treasured ring: a crochet, filet pattern doily, depicting hands folded in prayer. The sound of her tears lingered in the priest's ears as he rode from her farmhouse that day. They lingered in his ears even now, with the repetition of memory. He suppressed his agitation and forced himself to listen to the end of the old man's confession. Noon was approaching and Father Cosmo wanted desperately to refresh himself with a walk in the breezy garden. Then he would lunch with Signore Tojetti, who had gifts of elegantly bound books of poetry and philosophy. The seafood restaurant where they were to meet was just a few miles from the ocean. Father Cosmo enjoyed the smoothness of the sawdust-covered floors, the porthole mirrors above the bar, and the myriad photographs of ships at sea, which decorated the walls. He loved this church because of its proximity to the coast and the abundance of refreshing salt air.

"Do you think she sees my suffering? Can she know my sorrow? Can she know that I regret my shortcomings? That would be a great comfort, wouldn't it? Do you think she knows?"

Earlier this morning, before the first mass, while Father Cosmo was reading Signore Tojetti's letter, the cart driver had respectfully waited by the desk at the undertaker's office, after removing his filthy cap. The mortician had returned his pen to the inkwell as the child meekly lifted the imposing fedora to his glowering father as they began their weekly journey to church. Cases of suicide were handled with discretion, especially when the deceased was so young. The mortician, glad to conclude this unfortunate business, was grateful that the girl's parents were already at the cemetery, awaiting the arrival of the body for burial. After sending his assistant to get some carbolic acid, the mortician had spent a rather long time preparing the girl's body. He was respected in the town; many funerals were performed on account and there were many families who owed the man for billing the necessary dignified procedures on a monthly installment basis. Release papers had to be signed before the corpse could be dressed, placed into the coffin and transported. When the mortician came back upstairs he was flushed and distracted. He found it impossible to look at the driver face-to-face and stared at the man's boot when he spoke to him. As he rose from the desk to let the driver out and simultaneously admit the two men brought along to carry the box to the cart, another assistant struggled with the bluish-white, staring, rigid form that hours before had spoken and moved, trying to push the stiffened legs through a petticoat the way one would struggle with an undressed, uncooperative mannequin. The assistant recoiled in disgust when he tried to grip the girl's upper thigh. It was the driver who felt a personal affinity for the dead girl: like her and her family, he was a farmer and lived off the land.

The boy instinctively flinched as his father reached for the crumpled hat. Grasping the child's wrist with a practiced gesture, the man led him out of the church, the knotted rosary dangling from his other hand.

The sparrows remained on the branches. As Father Cosmo opened the door of the confessional and gingerly helped the old man to remove himself, the umbra of the perched birds vanished. The postern swung forward and dispelled the forms of sunlight like a mirrored closet door casting out its reflected occupants as it is opened. In fact Father Cosmo appeared to reach for a garment the way a person who is late vacantly regards an item of clothing, grabbing the old man's arm without noticing he was there. A moment later the sparrows actually leapt from their perch and flew towards the sea. Deprived of the interplay of light and shade, the confessional portal no longer recorded the birds' movement. Their departure from the branches included real, sudden, spiked motion of flapping wings. The old man struggled ahead, aided by Father Cosmo, with uncertain steps. At the altar the other priest prepared for the next mass as the horse's ears pricked to the cart driver's affectionate whistle. A large bump in the uneven dirt caused the small, pine casket to thud against the side of the cart as the blind young man stumbled into the sisters. Greatly fatigued from their difficult ascent to the final step of the church, they were dizzy and disoriented, and took no notice of the clicking stick that announced his approach.

At the church entrance, a breeze made the water in the font quiver slightly. The housekeeper anointed herself when the cart approached with its wooden cargo. She shook dust from her shawl. The particles swirled in the wind and seemed to blend with the sawdust from the cheap casket. The coffin jumped once more as the rear wheel of the cart suddenly dipped. At that moment the blacksmith, with his little boy in tow, looked back and saw Father Cosmo behind the lurching box as the priest took leave of the old man. A piece of crumpled paper, dangling from his cassock pocket, blew away suddenly. The sky had darkened and the moist air indicated a thunderstorm. The little paper bounced along the wooden floorboards until it became wedged between two flowerpots on display in front of the potter's store a short distance from the church. The potter's young apprentice raced back and forth as he brought the wares back into the shop so they would be safe from the imminent heavy rain. The widower and the wagon moved in opposite directions while Father Cosmo stood between them at the vaulted church entrance.

Standing by the open grave at the cemetery, the dead girl's father anxiously shuffled his fingers within the pocket of his trousers, making the few coins collected there tinkle softly. A mound of earth, about three feet high, stood on the side of the rectangular hole. The loss of his daughter, and particularly the realization that she was capable of taking her own life, was most disturbing to the man. The finality of what had happened continued to escape him; he was overwhelmed by a strange feeling of unreality, a detached, nebulous dream-state that preserved the living image of a dead loved one and somehow contradicted the certainty that that person will never be seen or heard again. Consequently, the man became very conscious of what he looked at and tried to avoid his daughter's casket placed on the side of the grave. The shovel was embedded in the loose earth. He looked beyond the cemetery at a lovely white house in the distance. There was a rain barrel on the right side of the porch and a little boy was chasing his dog down the steps. The man turned his head suddenly because the image of the child scooping up his puppy made him think in rapid sequence of past images of his daughter.

The grasshopper made a few jerky movements as two mockingbirds pecked it with quick, vigorous nods of their beaks. The old man tried to summon the strength for the walk back to his empty house. The thin legs of the insect twitched faintly as the birds took turns trying to lift it to their nest. Father Cosmo stared at this hideous display of nature's laws. The strong breeze wrapped the garden with the sensual aroma of the sea. The sight of this creature being eaten alive sickened the priest.

He looked away.

In the Forest

"I thought the forest murders were a cold case. Didn't the lead detective commit suicide?"

"That was a long time ago. I can't remember."

"I wanted to have a look at the transcript, the last interview with the man who admitted to the killings. Do you suppose all the records have been put into storage?"

"They're probably in the basement. They've been filed away for years. I don't know for sure. I can't remember. It really doesn't matter. That man got away. They threw out the confession. There was psychiatric testimony. They said that man was delusional. Psychotic. I think the diagnosis was that he suffered from multiple personality disorder. I'm not an expert but that's supposed to be a very rare condition. Anyway the dominant opinion held that the confession was coerced, phony, suspect, tainted. There was no trial. He was never convicted. I haven't spoken to anyone about the forest murders for years."

"You seem a little touchy about all this. I'm sorry because I'm new. I know I haven't been in the department as long as you. It's a famous case and I guess I'm just curious. Didn't you play a big role in it, too?"

"It's not your fault. I was engaged to one of the victims. She was the woman they found near the resort lodge. The one he clubbed to death with the chunk of marble from the fireplace. I had been on the case for six months. We couldn't find any real leads. They gave me medical leave for a short period when my fiancé was murdered. I was so deeply in love. I wasn't thinking very clearly after that. I used to stare at things all the time. I examined and studied the evidence countless times. The hammer. The shotguns. The hunting boots. The rabbit traps. The red jogging suit. The child's plastic identity card with the metal clasp. I examined the car over and over again. I went back to the resort lodge hundreds of times. The apartment, too. Everything. At one point we thought there might be several killers. The logical examination of an illogical event can withstand only so much contradiction. Things were duplicated, events overlapped. How could so many different victims get killed in an identical way in the same place? The whole timeline of the murders began to get confused, but somehow all the evidence always pointed to the forest. Everything led to the forest."

What's the point of keeping this goddamn journal if I don't have a smoke when I want one?! I need a smoke. I knew it wasn't an ordinary case. I didn't need a crystal ball to figure that out. Murder for profit or revenge or passion made sense. There's simplicity and logic to it. Like an engine, like a fire. If a husband blows his wife's brains out because he catches her with another guy, it isn't pretty but it certainly isn't surprising. But these forest murders just didn't make sense. Why would a man plan a killing in a place that would be swarming with kids from a field trip? Why would a perfectly responsible woman let a stranger into her apartment, especially when she had to prepare for a hunting trip with her father? Why would a jogger run along a path that was frequently littered with broken glass? Why would a murderer use a hunting knife, a garrote, and a shotgun when any one could have sufficed? This case was a bad one, all right. People don't like hearing about murders that don't make sense. Especially when it's gory and illogical and the victims are all young women and the only clear thing is that there's some deranged creature out there who's going to do it again and again until he's stopped. The more I looked at this case, the less I understood. The forest murders began after they transferred me from vice to homicide. I remember when I was in vice and you'd get some poor old junkie. For them old was around forty. Sometimes I'd find a poor bastard gazing at the sink or the wall or the floor with that weird transfixed look, like Bernadette's frozen stare, as if the stains of their own shit and puke and blood on the filthy floor were some kind of beatific road map revealing the secrets of the universe or something. The thing that always spooked me was that little fart of choked laughter you'd hear when you put the cuffs on. You'd have to carefully walk them down the cracked wooden steps because by this point the only thing holding them up was wishful thinking. I'd always look away when they'd turn around and gaze up at me with those empty eyes. Sometimes their voices were so raspy from years of junk that the words sounded like twigs snapping in a fire. I hated that. No, this certainly wasn't an ordinary case. That's the goods, all right. I started this journal to keep track of the questions, all the damn questions about the forest murders. The questions without answers; the questions that won't go away. Did the murderer plan the whole thing so it would look like the killing in the book we found near the car? Did the killer disguise himself as a hunter so he could move through the forest undetected? Was he the father of one of the boys on the school trip? I'm not convinced that the Law can help anymore. What about those tape recordings of all those poor kids screaming? It was that husband and wife abduction case. They used pliers on the children and recorded the torture sessions. Bitch chewed gum during the trial, filed her nails like a proud animal licking blood from its fur. I couldn't let it pass. I'm not supposed to stick around after I deliver the groceries. Why am I wasting my time with this? What's the use of writing this down when the words won't mean the same thing tomorrow? I've got a case to solve. I have to get out there.

Why did you commit the murder in the woods?

I always wanted to kill her in the forest. It had to be there. The thought never left my mind. I wanted it to be violent. Nature's violence.

Plant life devoured by insects, insects eaten by rodents, rodents captured by birds, birds shot by humans. I wanted to become a link in this chain of natural bloodshed. Lush surroundings. Ghostly trees. Tall. Very gaunt; very gnarled. Maze of paths choked with leaves. Chips of bark snagged in her hair as I rolled her limp body through the grass. Sharp twig ends were sucked into her nostrils. Blood mixed with mud. Blood sprayed across my hunting boots. Did I tell you that I was an experienced hunter? I was quite a sportsman. Deer; rabbit; duck especially. There was plenty of legal game in that forest, depending on the season.

Please stick to the questions. You were talking about her blood...

Blood in a fine spray speckled the last page of the book I had with me. Smooth and cold pebbles covered with warm blood. Not too far from my resort lodge. Then I could drag her back without too much bother. Never mind about the kids playing. My son was with the group. I wasn't expected for hours. I could find a way around that difficulty. Those field trips usually took up the entire school day. The forest is limitless.

Did you hear anything unusual when you killed her?

No. The kids from the school trip played wildly but I couldn't hear the metal clasps that connected the plastic identity cards to the elastic bands they wore around their necks. The clasps shook fitfully, every time the ball was thrown, every time the blindfold was fastened, but I couldn't see them, either. I did hear her gurgling throat. Desperate gasps for air. Her body shook like stones rattling in a metal box as she struggled to breathe.

When you were arrested, why did they find you thrusting your hands into the sky, as if you were trying to grab one of the birds flying above the resort lodge?

It was part of my overall sense of murderousness, the brute force I wanted to create and luxuriate in. I projected my arm with abruptness, the way I stabbed her, the way I shredded the soles of her feet with glass shards, the way I tightened the ligature made of rabbit trap nylon across her throat. I imagined the clatter of the shaking clasps, a clatter that was chaotic and unnerving.

What happened to the book you had with you?

I don't remember. It was covered with blood, smeared with mud. Nothing could remove the stains. I lost my place so many times that day. I know when I looked away from the birds it was that same page, it was always that same page, the one with the candid language of a detective writing in his diary, making a daily account of the case he was on. There was a gruesome description of a woman receiving a merciless, fatal beating. The detective knew she was already unconscious. He, in fact, was the killer. The book kept you guessing at it for a long time. The detective was insane; he used his knowledge and power to make the evidence point in all directions. He killed women who loved him. He was very cruel. His last victim had very slender arms, like stalks, like branches. Pure white skin splashed with blood from his fierce, continuous blows. He beat her with the hot brutality of an animal: savage, persistent, thorough. A chunk of the mantelpiece rested across her skull. He clubbed her with the marble after breaking it with his hammer. Her father stood with several friends in the photograph taken by the pond. Her blood spiraled down the glossy black and white picture, as though it dripped from the tips of the shotgun barrels.

The medical report revealed that your victim had been dead approximately ten hours by the time of your arrest. Do you recall at what time she lost consciousness?

The birds distracted me. They were frightened. They were too close to the pond, they could sense the danger of the raised guns. I didn't notice but I know she fainted at some point. Probably just after the mantelpiece shattered. A chip of marble lodged in her eye. The shock of the impact and the realization of what the detective planned to do must have been too much for her. The birds' departure startled me, a rapid movement of flapping wings. Like thunder claps, like faucets turned on full blast. I could see this. Just as I propelled my arms to grab the metal clasps, to stop them from shaking. But I had already looked away from the sky. I lowered my eyes from the birds to the page of the book where the clatter of the clasps was described, the clatter that couldn't be heard. I projected my arm with jerky energy, with a clenched bloody fist that descended upon her slender white arms already bloodied by my fierce blows. A knock at the door?! Was she expecting visitors? I must wash out the blood. I must leave quickly.

What about the jogger?

Somebody was out there running. He was testing his endurance, trying to cover the whole forest. The sound of his loud footfalls blended into the din produced by the jangling clasps. He saw dark blurry forms, like shafts, like trees. As he ran, these forms passed in rapid succession, lined in rows on his left and right. They must have been trees. Hundreds of noisy sparrows perched among the branches. Their chirping drowned out the remote dissonance of the hunters' duck calls in the distance. The combination of artificial and natural bird noise almost obliterated the police sirens that prompted me to leave the blood-splattered apartment. He was wearing a bright red jogging suit. The deep red glowed with sunshine, with fall colors, as if it were burning, as if he were incandescent, luminous, it was as if the sturdy, straight pine trees wobbled and swayed, affected by the burning, by the brightness. There were slivers of glass strewn throughout the road. An angry hunter had spitefully shattered some camp lanterns. The jogger ran at a measured pace. Occasionally tiny pieces of glass became embedded in the rubber soles of his running shoes.

Do you think the jogger or the hunter saw you at any point?

It's possible. Anything is possible in the forest. My furious movements, my nervous gestures, snapping my arm out suddenly, screaming at the top of my lungs: none of this drowned out the sound of the approaching man, so I continued to beat the woman. I knew the jogger was still deep in the forest and couldn't interfere with the crime. The silent shaking clasps had become a blur, a confusion of dizzying motion. There was a vertical row of buttons on each child's jacket. Some were on the left, some on the right, like shafts, like trees. I had an image of running feet, swift movements, glass splinters imbedded in the intact, firm trees, hundreds of startled, chirping sparrows. The bright red jogging suit was extremely tight, excessively tight, a stinging tightness which cut into the jogger's flesh.

Your feet were bleeding too, weren't they? Hadn't they been cut in some unusual way?

Yes. They were in very bad shape by that point. In spite of this I had reached the top of a steep hill. When I looked down I saw all the red leaves stuck to the razor-edged Black Needle Rush points lining the slope on both sides. And I know on that day of hunting in that very forest her father must have realized how easily these leaves could be pierced by the plants' dry thorns: the moment before the photograph was taken, a flock of birds pierced the sky with equal precision, equal sharpness, the leather-thick flapping of their wings heard by all but not included by the lens. The shock of wing noise almost made me lose balance and fall from the hill. All the cuts I received made me lose a great deal of blood. When I lowered my arm I noticed several drops of my blood falling past. The dripping blood partially obscured the image of the white birds. I heard shotgun fire as I stabbed her. Distant, muffled, like faraway thunder, faraway waterfalls. The hot blood, the driving blade hitting bone, the racing ants showered with intestinal fluids, the severity of the barrels, the red metal of the guns, the overlapping knots of the tree roots, the frenzy of nature's energy: I slung out my arm, fiercely directing it toward one of the white, convulsing, blood stained forms.

It must have been quite a struggle to reach the top of the hill.

More than a struggle. It was a feat of endurance. An exhibition of stamina. And when the jogger finally reached the peak, he glanced back. Black Needle Rush (Juncus roemerianus) plants lined the slope. Their inflexible projections had shredded his feet. The tight running suit would not stretch against the movement of his body. The bright garment, glowing in the golden autumn sunlight, was speckled with sticky red leaves. Trying to stand at the top of the hill, his balance was disturbed by the shocking flap of multiple bird wings. Dizziness accompanied his blood loss, and the numerous cuts which caused the bleeding made him understand that the Black Needle Rush points were like tiny spears, allowing the plants to harpoon objects such as leaves which might somehow come into contact with them. He heard multiple shotgun fire in the distance, a muffled volley of shots which must certainly kill several white birds, causing blood drops to fall past those white forms. The red metal of the barrels, the explosions they produced: the fury of it all made him whip out his arm, in the manner of a very precise callisthenic gesture, muscles tightened and overlapping like tree knots, like marble veins. He fiercely projected his arm. He wanted to become part of the destructiveness of the shotguns. The long guns were lifted suddenly, swung to the right, and fired. They created explosions that penetrated the distance, reverberating beyond the targets. He focused on this extraordinary violence from afar. He saw the savage redness of the barrels. The hunter searched the nearby bushes, hoping to find a number of dead birds. He had promised his daughter an early start on their weekend camping trip, and he would like to make a good showing in the hunt in order not to be embarrassed when the group photograph was taken. He was very annoyed: his fire brought down only one bird. He squatted beside the limp, bloodied form. His anger mounted over having shot so poorly all day. In frustration he thrust out his arm in a quick, impatient manner, picking up the bird and hastily flinging it into the bag. He raised his eyes from the spot where he had retrieved his game. He looked at the darkening sky where many other birds continued flying, as if in mockery of his inferior marksmanship. He found it unusual to see so much of the flock still in the area, in spite of the casualties already inflicted by the gunfire. I closed my book and prepared to leave. The approaching hunters and the swift accumulation of rain clouds convinced me that this afternoon of reading was about to come to an end.

Were you still reading that same page?

I must have been. It was always the same page, the one with the impassioned description of the red gun barrels smoking in the distance, producing noise that penetrated far into the forest, creating vibrations that shook nearby bushes in which I hoped to find some dead birds. I was always searching for something in the forest. I would never leave the forest. I searched the apartment, looking for the shotguns that had been recklessly fired. I was distressed to discover that my hammer cracked the marble in one place only. I wanted several pieces to beat her with and my anger mounted over having overlooked so many bloodstains. I squatted beside her bloody form, lying at my feet in the final moments before death. I sharply extended my arm towards the bird, picking it up and angrily flinging it into my game bag. I found it unusual that the doors to the neighboring apartments remained shut in spite of her horrific screams moments before, not to mention the darkening sky where many birds continued to fly. So I closed my book and prepared to leave: the spot previously occupied by the shot animal, and the sudden accumulation of rain clouds, convinced me that the hunter's fire brought down only one bird. The business of this afternoon was about to be concluded.

What happened after you finished the last page?

Some of the words were the same, they were repeated from paragraph to paragraph, but many of the words were different. I didn't notice the flecks of mud on the sleeve of my khaki jacket. I raised my eyes from the bloody corpse and glanced at the clock on the nearby desk. Seeing the time, I realized I must leave very soon: the dead woman had expected visitors and someone might knock at the door at any moment. First I washed the blood from my hands, and then I changed into the fresh clothes I had brought. I nervously scoured my hands in the sink. The hot water gushed from the faucet with great force. When the shotgun fire subsided, the jogger looked up at the sky, watching the flock of frightened birds. Returning to my book, I glanced at my sleeve and became annoyed when I saw the mud. I knew very well it would not wash out. I raised my eyes from the bloodied corpse, turning to the last page of the book. Seeing the time, I realized that a few flecks of mud were on the left sleeve of my khaki jacket. After the shotgun fire subsided, the hunter became annoyed at the clock on the marble mantelpiece. He must leave very soon because the sink had not been washed clean. Water shot from the faucet as he looked at the woman who was certainly dead by now. At any moment someone might enter the apartment and change into the fresh clothes he had brought with him. Before that happened, he would wash the blood from his sleeve. He was expecting visitors, and he was quite annoyed to see the flock of frightened birds. I decided to spend that afternoon jogging in the forest. I was in no mood to entertain guests. Totally inconsiderate of those who expected to find me home, I left early in the morning without notifying anyone of my change in plans.

"Sorry to hear that. It must have been tough for you, losing the woman you loved. You were able to work on the case, though. That must have given you a little satisfaction. Was it tough holding on to some hope that you could catch him?"

"The thought never left my mind. I tracked down everybody. The hunter, the jogger, the group of children, the resort lodge owner, even the author of the book that was found. None of it ever led anywhere. Most of the bodies were discovered during the summer months, when there were lots of hunting parties in the forest. We detained and questioned everybody. The Captain was worried about me. Officially

I had been taken off the case, for obvious personal reasons. The Captain let me do my own interviews, my own investigation, off the record, so to speak. He knew I was losing my perspective, though. I would go maybe four or five days without sleep. I had nightmares when I slept so I drank coffee all the time. I remember the nightmares very clearly. I was running through the forest. It began to rain suddenly. The rain hurt. It was heavy and cold and the sheets of water cut into me. I was being flayed as I ran because the water was sharp and it sliced off parts of my body. I was drenched in blood but I kept going. I could see myself running from across the road. I could see myself from the vantage point of the many trees that lined the road. Finally I became a skeleton, a fleshless thing charging through the forest, like something out of an old ghost story. After my fiancée was murdered, I lost my way. I don't remember sleeping at all. I spent weeks looking at photographs of her. Places we had been. I used to kid her about a photograph she had taken with her father. She was a hunter, like her old man. I told her she looked cute in her hunting outfit, the camouflage gear, floppy hat like Elmer Fudd."

It's almost 10pm. Somehow we got a lead that the killer might be making films of the girls. Snuff movies, torture movies, sick shit. A pal of mine in vice did a raid and wound up with some films like that. Some of our victims were mature women, but some were younger, a few runaways, too. There were two who fit the age and description of the runaways who disappeared and wound up on those god-forsaken films. I found the bastard who trafficked in those movies and left him standing on a stack of wobbly phone books with the noose around his neck and his hands tied behind his back. If he didn't choke himself by the time I get back down there, maybe he'll have a different story to tell me about some of the new girls. It started to rain while I drove across town to get something to eat. I thought it was funny how I could almost see his hands wriggling as the wipers swept the rain off the windshield. I like storms. They give me a weird energy, in spite of the gloom.

The questions won't go away. Are the killings cult inspired? Why are so many things red? The jogging suit, the car, the shotguns. Whoever heard of red shotgun barrels? How does a man beat a woman to death, then stab her dozens of times, then strangle her, then blow her apart with a shotgun, and remain undetected for an entire afternoon in a place where joggers and hunters and school children are all less than a couple of hundred yards from one another? Got to find out what's behind this. I don't plan on disappointing anybody. I spent enough time in the butcher clinic with the coroner. I saw enough of what this psycho did to the two other girls. I don't like counting unrecognizable bodies. I don't like having to tell the parents that we need DNA to make a positive I. D. because the bodies don't have faces anymore. I got a few ideas about this case. I know what to do. I trust my instincts. Better that way. No reason to explain anything until the time comes. I'll keep things to myself for now.

So no one knew you would be in the forest?

Of course not. I had planned to kill her that day. I quickened my pace from time to time, darting off in a sprint for about two hundred yards. I felt good. I knew my plan was sound. I made a rapid mental inventory as I ran. I remembered everything. I remembered a recent dream in which I passed some children from a field trip playing blind man's bluff at the bottom of a valley, but for the most part I ran on the main road, lined on both sides with dark oak trees. As I passed the children, one of them looked up. He must have seen me. Because of the distance and the speed of my movements, one of the children saw me only for an instant. I was no more than a blur which quickly lost its hold on the child's attention. The road was littered with broken glass and other debris. It was useless for the hunter to continue searching that area: he knew his fire brought down no other birds. So with complete disregard for those who expected to spend an afternoon jogging, the hunter spontaneously increased his pace, darting off in a sprint for several hundred yards. He ran on the main road, lined on both sides with groups of playing children. He decided that one of the children saw him only for an instant. And he left quite early, without even bothering to tell the others that he would be at the bottom of a valley. But as he passed the children one of them happened to look up and find him home. Because he was in no mood to entertain guests, he was no more than a blur. It was useless to continue searching the area, mainly because of the distance and the speed with which I ran through the forest. My gunfire lost its hold on the child's attention. No other birds caught a glimpse of me, running on the main road littered with broken glass.

Was the hunter very bitter that day?

Uncontrollably. Scowling at the empty game bag, he hastily wiped the blood from his hands as he contemplated the now impossible timetable he must follow in order to pick up his daughter at the appointed hour. Droplets of rain were already falling, adding to the disgust and frustration he felt over this day of fruitless hunting which was about to end. The last page of his book had become a little soggy. He ignored this for the moment: he was anxious to finish the story, and he didn't think the rain would come down too heavily just then. The book was meant as a birthday gift for his daughter, a popular murder mystery. The steady beads of rain had moistened the mud spots on his sleeve. The dry earth dissolved into thin lines which streamed down the khaki fabric. The jogger dried his hands, he washed out the sink with hot water, he wiped the blood from the burglar tools, he listened for footsteps in the hallway. Gradually the blood disappeared from the sink, the last red traces obliterated by the steady splashes of very hot water. He thought of everything. Yet in spite of his preparedness he was foolish to ignore what appeared to be only superficial wounds: he was unable to run any farther, in fact he could barely walk. He sat down at the top of a hill and tried to summon new strength. Meanwhile the children grew impatient with the distracted behavior of one particular boy: they wanted him to return to their game, to exhibit the same enthusiasm he had manifested earlier in the day. The boy lowered his eyes from the top of the hill and gazed at his friends who were so anxiously concerned with his participation in their fun.

Did the hunter manage to keep his appointment?

I'm not sure. I was in the final stage of the murder and my mind was elsewhere. I had a huge combat knife with a very wide blade. Little reflected pieces of the scene flitted across the shiny metal. The shotgun blasts shattered the marble into a thousand pieces. As I dragged her body I heard the birds overhead. They flew above her corpse, casting waves of shadow over her nude bloody form, like rippling nets, like swaying leaves. I was very angry when I glanced at the empty game bag. I ignored the soggy last page of the book. Drops of cold rain made me regard my muddy sleeve with disgust. My hands were moistened by the light but steady beads of rain, so I wiped off the remains of the blood. I was anxious to conclude that ridiculous day of hunting. I didn't think the rain would stream in thin lines along the khaki fabric of my jacket. I dried my hands. I washed out the superficial wounds. Lowering my eyes from the top of the hill, I could see the splashing, extremely hot water. Gradually the blood disappeared down the drain, although traces of it remained upon the thorny plants lining the hill. And I was foolish to ignore my friends. I was unable to run any farther, I couldn't even walk. My distracted behavior was about to end. It was time to think about the resort lodge, the best path to use in dragging her body there, the timetable I needed in order to meet my daughter on schedule, the plastic sheets I had left in the backseat of my car, the sheets I would use to wrap her body, the excuse I planned to give my daughter, to explain my lateness. The field trip playmates, previously so concerned with the boy's participation in their fun, seemed oblivious to his exhaustion. They ran about in the sunlight while he stood in shadow. He had perspired from running around so much, and with the air becoming chilly he decided to button his jacket. The gradual accumulation of large, dark clouds blotted out the sun, and he realized that it would rain very soon. His playmates were engaged in their game and, unlike him, they had not buttoned their jackets; they seemed unaffected by the cool air. I don't think they had perspired as profusely as I, and therefore they did not feel the least bit chilled. Raising my eyes, I looked at the sky. I saw several birds flying away from the trees. Then I looked from the sky to the little spots of dried blood on the palm of my right hand. Earlier a rude jogger accidentally shoved me and I scraped my hand against the ground. The burning pain of that injury in addition to the clear sign of a furious rainstorm convinced me that I should leave the forest.

Was it very cloudy and dark by the time you killed her?

A jumble of leaf shadows surrounded the boy because he remained under a large tree. The air had turned cool and his young friends ran about in the sunlight. The accumulating rain clouds gradually blotted out the sun. The boy realized that it would rain very soon but, unlike himself, his playmates had perspired. And for a moment he thought about raising his eyes from their jackets and looking up at the sky. He buttoned his own jacket while several birds were peacefully floating across the sky. However, the birds did not move as quickly as the trickle of blood across his right hand. Lowering his eyes from the little spots of blood on his playmates, he looked at the burning pain received from a downpour. Earlier, one of his friends had lacerated the ground. He did not wish to remain in the area because of this irritation.

What about the words on the last page of the book?

I read them with feverish anticipation. This was the denouement, where, many years after the murders, the detective broke down for some inexplicable reason and let a newcomer see the truth. It must have been the cumulative effect of the detective's questionable emotional state, his derangement. It was finally revealed that, by assuming the identities of some of the key figures from the case who were questioned, the detective hoped to cast suspicion elsewhere. But before I turned to the last page, I stopped for a moment to try to remember where I had parked my car. The unforeseen noise of the shotguns made me think of the location of the red automobile. Instantly I recalled that I had parked just off the main road, approximately two hundred yards to the right of the resort lodge. There was no cause for alarm. Even in the event of rain, indicated by the darkening sky, it was not difficult to locate the vehicle. My only concern was that the dark clouds and the late hour might impede my progress, perhaps making me lose my way. Remembering that some time long ago I had gotten lost in this forest under similar circumstances, I naturally didn't want a repetition of that situation. I continued reading, thinking that I heard the distant sound of someone running, but at that point I was much too absorbed in the ending of the book to pay any attention to such a vague sound.

Did you hear voices when you killed her? Did you hear or smell strange things that day? Can you hear me? Do you want to take a break?

I read feverishly for only a moment or two, desperately trying to remember where I parked my car. The shock of the shotgun blasts made me think of the last page of my book. Before I turned to that page, I stopped the bright red automobile. I decided there was no cause for alarm: I could park just off the main road. The clouds hovered to the right of the resort lodge. And the spot I was in wouldn't be difficult to locate, even in the event of rain, a factor which under similar circumstances would make me lose my way. But the more I read the more I thought that some time long ago I had been totally absorbed by the sound of someone running, and that the runner's concern was whether or not his sounds would impede my progress. I paid no attention to the darkening sky. I was so exasperated by the small number of birds I had shot, I completely lost track of my friends, still busy retrieving their own game. I stood up and removed my long hunting knife from its sheath. I wanted to inspect the ground. The blade was very sharp and I nearly cut myself as I held it in my hand. I laid down my shotgun. I cut loose all the empty rabbit traps I had set earlier in the day. My impatience and frustration made me careless. Most of the stab wounds were too deep: I could not catch the blood and I deprived myself of the pleasure of watching her die slowly. I thought of the agony of the trapped rabbits, the shot birds, the captured insects, the hunted mice. The traps were now useless; I had cut them out of the bush too hastily. This didn't concern me at all. My only desire at that point was to leave the forest as soon as possible. And with good reason. I was so completely annoyed by the poor number of birds I had shot that I stood up and removed my long hunting knife from its sheath. And before I examined the ground, I lost track of my friends still busy retrieving their own game. The blade was very sharp. I cut myself. I held the empty rabbit traps in my hands. My shotgun rendered them useless. Earlier in the day I laid down my impatience, my exasperation. By this point my only desire was to leave the forest as soon as possible.

Can you hear me? Do you want me to call for the doctor?

Everybody was in a weakened state. No one wanted to remain in the forest after dark. It was idiotic of us not to tell anyone we would be here. We had already lost a great deal of blood. Now we weren't sure if we could make it back to the main road. Certainly it was too late to expect other joggers and hunters who, like ourselves, might've ventured this far into the woods. We managed to stand up, walking feebly but steadily ahead. If we continued at this pace, we might reach the road in about two hours (if we were lucky). But we were foolish to remain in the forest after dark. We were too weak; we didn't want to tell anyone. Other joggers had already lost a great deal of blood. They didn't know if I would make it. Certainly it was too late to expect to walk steadily ahead. I managed to stand up. I had ventured far into the woods. If I continued at that pace, I would proceed only feebly. At that moment my leg started to act up again. I knew I had to get out of that apartment as quickly as possible. Having committed the murder, my confidence swiftly evaporated. Now I leapt across the bloodstained corpse, running as fast as possible. My footsteps echoed loudly in the long empty hallway as I cursed the slow elevator. And with my leg ablaze with pain, my confidence was shaken. Having completed my crime, I knew I had to leave the apartment as quickly as possible. I cursed the slowness of my footsteps. The elevator seemed to take forever to reach the blood stained corpse. The hallway echoed loudly as I leapt across the bloody blanket of sparrows and rabbits. The boy rejoined his friends, already climbing the hill, eager to return home. The rain clouds had finally burst, and the water streamed down heavily. He knew they could all run for cover to a nearby resort lodge, owned by the father of one of his friends. He realized he would be the last to leave; his own father was not supposed to come for him until much later. But in the meantime he could join his friends, already climbing the hill. Eager to return home, the rain streamed down heavily. The boys' playmates realized that they would be the last to leave. They knew that their fathers were not supposed to run to a nearby resort lodge. I saw my car as I rushed through the pouring rain. Not intending to wander off when I did, I had left the motor running, and I heard the car's vibrating body. I could see the car. I ran towards it in the pouring rain. I hadn't expected to wander through the forest, and I had left the motor running. I could see the car's vibrating body. I found the bloody hunting knife next to the fender, sandwiched between the pages of the book. I withdrew the knife and wiped the blood from the blade. I could see another forest reflected on the bright metal. In that forest was another book, and another bloody knife between its pages.

"No wonder this case got so much publicity. The strain on you guys must have been horrible. Your partner must have had it pretty bad, the guy who killed himself. Pardon me for asking, but did he kill himself when the suspect was released?"

"I didn't have a partner. I was the only one assigned to this case. It was my case. It belonged to me. It would always be my case. There can't be any doubt about that. I suppose they think that if they keep playing their little game and constantly put people like you in my path, I'll finally give in and admit that there's nothing left to solve. I know better. I am not going to give up. I visit her grave every night. I loved her so. She's buried somewhere in the forest. There's a cemetery. It is very old. I know where the headstone is but I need markers to guide myself. I can always ask one of the hunters if I lose my way. Maybe the people in the resort lodge will let me stop and rest for a little bit. I'm very tired these days. I think I need to sleep. I've been working too hard. I shouldn't overtax myself with all that exercise. Running is supposed to be good for the cardiovascular system. I think shooting defenseless birds should not be a sport. It is a sick amusement for those who do not value the preciousness of life. I know how important life is. I would not harm a bird. I gave up that wretched hobby long ago when I had a bad dream about all the birds dying simultaneously. I could not find my game bag and the image of the dying birds filled my mind and I ran away in shame. I do like movies. I saw a documentary about the underworld and how murders are often filmed for huge profits."

I know about that. I have to talk to that guy who we suspect. He gets films like that. I put it in my journal last night so I wouldn't forget. It's on page... I forgot the page but I know I wrote it down. So this morning we hauled in Flicker Frankie for some routine ball breaking. Runs a porno parlor downtown but we know he gets the young stuff. It's always timing that screws things up because he's a clever bastard. He knows what to hide and when to hide it, like a worm burrowing into fresh mud. He's a human sore. If they'd let me I'd kill him so slowly you'd need time elapse photography to figure out how his body got like that. There's information out there and I have to get it before another woman dies. Confident prick sits there arranging his lard-slick hair with a stainless steel comb. I don't deal no under age stuff, he says. I ain't about to let nobody search nothin' without a warrant, he says. You got probable cause? You got a charge? I got a business to run. Yeah he's got a business, all right. The wretched lives of some abused runaway kids get knocked down into the slime a few more notches when they do a little of Frankie's business on a stained mattress in front of a few cameras. Just some warm-ups before the street life kicks into high gear. Right there in the middle of the interrogation room I wanted to cut him open. Right there I wanted to pluck his eyes out of his head and stuff them down his wretched throat. I don't suppose they'd let me include it in the report. I heard the old stairway creak under Frankie's fat ass as he walked out of the station. Plenty of stories that won't go away about some kind of a cult that imports women for weird sex rites and I'm convinced that ton of shit is a middle-man for the trade. FBI boys "volunteered" one of their cute ass psycho profiles and they're into the idea of a lone hunter. That could be, too. Hunter and prey, ancient stuff, it's burned into our genes and we're trained through life to discard the urges but deep down the original impulse is still alive. I've been going through a few things on anthropology. The Egyptian stuff in particular, plenty of rites of the dead, that weird resurrection symbol. Who knows? Maybe there's a lead here, something I've been missing...I don't want to miss anything...I have to be thorough...where's the journal?...time to write it all down...don't want to forget anything...very important...who knows for sure who's killing these women?...got to find out...write it all down...write it all down...there's always a certainty of some kind when you write something down...I saw the film...there was a killing...some kind of strange ritual...I was wearing a hunter's outfit...they gave me the large knife...I heard stones rattling...it was all very hypnotic...like water falling...they made the film in the forest...the jogger was a rich businessman...he owned a resort lodge there...they told me to do it...I liked the way she gurgled on her blood...let me alone...let me alone...

CRIME SCENE EVIDENCE [ITEM NO. 30]

LAST PAGE OF NOVEL FOUND NEXT TO VEHICLE IN THE FOREST

His insanity had been growing all the time, like a stubborn weed, and the papers and the media had feasted off it. He had fooled everyone. Now it was over. He was glad. The murders in his mind were like being sick on a case of bad scotch while you stumble through a funhouse. It was like being rolled inside a blood soaked rug while you scream in a nightmare. No matter what angle he used to look at it, everything turned into another mirrored box, another secret room, nothing that was for sure, like shadows on the walls of an opium parlor. It was like fog sneaking into corners, bending its milky fingers, circling every tree in the forest, leading you nowhere all the time. A Merry-Go-Round of hooded figures pointing the way and everything just keeps going in circles. On some magical island paradise the Law does its exotic, perfumed dance, but from where he sat the Law was a scarecrow flying into your bloodstream, brandishing hatchets and poison darts; a chunk of raw meat riddled with maggots, spitting up bile, insane, savage. A nightmare sucking oxygen out of the air. A disfigured pancreas floating through Hell. No. There was no Law for him. There was only the need to kill women. They confiscated his gun and his badge. He was under arrest. His lips formed a twisted smirk like a deranged Halloween pumpkin. He knew there would always be something to harvest in the forest.

www.ingramcontent.com/pod-product-compliance
Ingram Content Group UK Ltd.
Pitfield, Milton Keynes, MK11 3LW, UK
UKHW041314190726
13845UKWH00025B/260

9 789363 543126